VBM

———

VALUE BASED MANAGEMENT

FOR

ACCOUNTS RECEIVABLE

BY

Kimberly Don Ketron

"Profitability in receivables lies in the value of the return, not the age of the debt."
-Kimberly Don Ketron

Contact me at:

kimberlyketron.com

Value Based Management For Accounts Receivable

The Purpose of This Book

The purpose of this book is to help businesses improve their profitability by improving the performance of their accounts receivable departments. While this book does include a basic overview of an insightful, value based collections technique, it is not a 'how to collect past due balances' book; it is instead a book that teaches how to manage accounts receivable for the optimal financial profit. The methods described in this book are for either business-to-consumer or business-to-business client based companies, although the majority of the focus is on business-to-business.

Utilization of VBMAR (Value Based Management for Accounts Receivable) works for the small, single mom-and-pop type store to the larger, multi-state, million dollar corporations. These methods will work in the receivables department but they can also be adapted to work in any department because the methods on a basic level apply a profitability mentality to the work approach.

What this book will not do is offer instruction on how to make debt collection phone calls, nor will it instruct on how to draft a past due notice. Anyone who is already in business already knows how to do that and to read a book on that is wasting time.

This book is more of an advanced user manual meant for those who are already up and running with accounts receivable but need or desire to improve their profitability, which should be everyone. What this book will do is offer some solid techniques that will improve what is already in place. Profit is the bottom line and the bottom line to any business and that bottom line is not created by the product mark-up. It has to do with enriching the customer's experience in dealing with the company from beginning to end. It is obvious to focus great attention in customer service techniques up front in terms of profiling the company, making the sale and building business relationships. However, additionally placing that focus on accounts receivable will improve profitability by bringing in the money on the back end, which is the deadly end to revenues. It is one thing to have a good accounts receivable balance that can be counted on as a business asset, but it is another thing entirely to actually have that cash on hand in order to utilize it for the business cash flow. That is what this book intends to do. Put the cash back into the business' receivables.

-Kimberly Don Ketron

CHAPTER ONE - Give Credit Where Credit Is Due

Why Extend Credit At All?

Imagine the average consumer with a shopping cart full of groceries, standing in line at the check out counter to make their purchases of food and household products. This transaction is accounts receivable to that store; but it is a simple and direct condition, the consumer pays and the store receives. There are no billings or credit terms.

No billings and no credit terms - in the day-to-day activities of the business world, this is not practical. In order for business vendors to reach their sales goals, they must be willing to extend credit. That means, they allow the customer to walk out with the goods (or they deliver the goods to the customer) and bill them later. This is not even the same as it would be if the consumer gave the grocery store clerk a credit card to pay for their goods, it would be more like them taking their groceries home and getting a paper bill for them later with thirty days to pay. Does this sound dangerous? The grocery store would think so.

There is one main advantage and one main disadvantage to selling on credit. On the advantage side, selling on credit will boost sales. This is because customers need to be able to buy things on credit in order to control cash flow and manage their businesses effectively. However, on the disadvantage side, it does expose the creditor to risk.

Proper credit management is extremely important because if too much credit is offered to the clients, it will cost in terms of investment in and maintenance of the accounts receivable. At the same time, offering too little credit will hinder profitability and sales. VBM is about finding that perfect balance. Remember that accounts receivable will create both direct and indirect costs, and therefore maximizing profitability concerning accounts receivable relies on effective credit management.

Anyone who is in business will have been running their own company or department, perhaps for a while, and will seem to have a set of receivables procedures that work; even those who are new to the field of credit management, will likely have ideas already on how to handle the business' credit. No one knows their business better than themselves. Even so, remember that in reality, the goal is not to just stay afloat and make a profit, the goal is to increase that profitability to the maximum state that it can become, and sometimes that just is not done with sales and marketing, sometimes it has to be cone by reducing the amount of default receivables. The first and most important, if not the step to doing this is establishing a good credit policy.

Establishing A Good Credit Policy

Most everyone already knows what credit is and how it works. Chances are most people had their first experience with credit back in college or maybe even in high school. Also, most all companies will likely already have had a credit and collection policy in place at their business. There will not be any time wasted here explaining the basics of credit like other accounts receivables how-to books do; instead, this book will skip to what is most important.

The key to accounts receivables is not the collections effort; the keys are the account set up and credit policies. If the business does not extend credit to those who do not pay their bills then the business will not have any problems. It is that simple.

The Most Commonly Made Credit Mistake

WRONG = Two companies with the same credit score receive the same credit limit.

Within most companies, a credit policy is set and standard. All new accounts being set up are ran through the same steps to determine credit worthiness. That is wrong. While credit personnel will perform the same steps on each new account application, they will not treat the results the same.

RIGHT = Two companies with the same credit score may receive two very different credit limits, because they are two very different companies with very different probabilities of payment.

Depending on which credit bureau is used, the credit ratings will come back on a scale either in the hundreds or on a scale of 1 to 100. For the purpose of this explanation, a more simplified credit scale will be created.

From now on, within the pages of this book, credit ratings are on a scale of 1 to 10. A company who has a credit rating of 10 has perfect credit and a company that has a credit rating of 1 has the poorest credit, deserving no credit.

Most companies have a predetermined credit limit scale that assigns a credit limit for a new customer based on the credit score they received on that company. For example, anyone with a 10 credit rating gets $5,000. Anyone with an 8 or 9 rating will get $3,000. Anyone with a 6 or 7 rating will get $2,000. Anyone with a 5 may get a credit limit of $500. Anyone with a credit rating of 4 or less is denied a credit account.

When credit limits are determined this way, it should be regarded that Company A who had a score of 9 pays better than Company B who also had a score of 9. Why is this so? If they both have good credit ratings, then why are their payment histories so different? Why does Company B consistently pay late? The answer to that question is one of the key secrets that will work to improve the accounts receivable profitability.

How a company pays their bills has less to do with their credit rating or the credit limit assigned to them and more to do with the value the vendor is to them. This is a very overlooked and obvious fact.

That is important enough to be repeated: how a company pays their bills has less to do with their credit rating or the credit limit assigned to them and more to do with the value the vendor is to them.

For example, let us talk about Company A and Company B, referenced above. Let us say that Company A is dental office and Company B is a hobby store. Now let us say the vendor is a nitrous oxide distributor.

Company A and Company B both apply for credit with the vendor. The vendor goes through the standard background and verification checks and runs the credit reports. Both Company A and Company B have a credit score of 9. Should the vendor give both Company A and Company B a credit limit of $3,000? Most companies would. That is a mistake.

The reason that it is a mistake is that the vendor does not hold the same value to the day-to-day operations of Company B that it does to Company A.

Company A will hold the vendor's services to being a higher value than company B and therefore it is more important to Company A that they stay in good standing with the vendor than it is to Company B. Company A is a dental office that needs nitrous oxide every day in order to medicate their patients. Company B only uses the nitrous oxide once a year, for example, during their model rocket promotional sales event. Company B could take up to a year to pay the vendor's invoice; it does not matter to Company B because they are not going to be calling the vendor next month for more nitrous oxide. Therefore, the vendor cannot hold up Company B's business. Hold up business to Company A who requires that delivery from that vendor almost daily.

Moving forward with this example, allow the assumption that both Company A and Company B have a bill from this vendor for nitrous oxide that is due tomorrow for $500 and both Company A and Company B also have another bill from a different vendor unrelated for the same amount of $500 for the delivery of glue, also due tomorrow. Both Company A and Company B only have $500 to pay a bill with today. That $500 worth of glue for the dental office, Company A, is simply office supplies that will last them all year. However, that $500 worth of glue to the model store, Company B, is only their weekly inventory of glue, one of their highest selling items and they cannot afford to have that stock running low. Which bill will each company choose to pay? It is obvious that Company A will pay the bill for nitrous oxide but Company B will pay the bill for glue.

In this particular case, it would be ok to give Company A the full $3,000 limit. Company B should only receive a quarter to a third of that amount, which equates to the amount of product they actually order.

Company A has more incentive in making sure they pay the nitrous oxide vendor on time because they do not want to be put on credit hold, which would be bad. Their customers would not have nitrous oxide and they could not perform their dental services.

Value Based Management For Accounts Receivable

Company B however, if they take all year to pay the nitrous oxide vendor that is of no concern, they do not need nitrous oxide again for 12 whole months. Being on credit hold with that vendor will not affect their business one bit. Companies will pay the vendor who has higher value to them first. The nitrous oxide vendor may not be paid from Company B for 30 to 60 or even 90 days outside of terms. By setting Company B's limit low, the nitrous oxide vendor reduces their risk and exposure. In a situation such as this, it is also good credit practice to require Company B to give a down payment on the nitrous oxide delivery. It should be assessed what the profit margin is on the delivery to Company B and use that to determine what down payment is asked for. The larger the profit margin, the lower the down payment that will be asked for; the smaller the profit margin, the higher the down payment that will be asked for. Always cover costs at the bare minimum.

Another strategy to use on Company B is to call them 5 or 10 days before the bill is due to remind them of the due date and make sure there are no issues preventing payment. At this time, ask them it can be asked if next year's order can be put in now, offer them a discount to do so, for the pre-order. The reason for this is to remind them that although they do not need the nitrous oxide services often, they will require those services again in the future. Offering the discount on next year's bill while this year's bill is still in front of them will put into their minds the idea of expenditure savings, which will incentivize a good business manager to follow through with the offer. However, do not take the order and extend the discount for next year until this year's bill is paid.

It is also advisable to use last year's sale to Company B as a reference to adjust their credit terms before sending them nitrous oxide again this year. When Company B calls the vendor and says it is time for their nitrous oxide again, the vendor can remind Company B of how many days they took to pay for the nitrous oxide last year and lower either their limit or set additional fees in place for late payments that might occur again this year.

Value Based Management For Accounts Receivable

Vendors should concentrate on getting paid by the customer while they are still a value to that customer. This is easier to do for continual ordering customers, and jobs that require progress payments. However, what about a customer who is only going to order one time? Should that vendor sell to them on net 30, deliver the product and then hope for payment a month later? Whether or not any vendor will sell to them on net 30 is that vendor's decision; but what they should most certainly do is ensure they are paid while they are still a value to that one time ordering customer. Cover costs, always. Require a down payment that meets costs or an earnest deposit before the one time delivery the goods. While making these decisions, keep in mind who the customer is, as well as what the potential profitability and future business from them might be. Every action within the bill collection genre that is performed should be done so with sales in mind.

Determining The Credit Terms

A payment policy is not a wish list. Every business owner would like to receive 100 percent cash on the barrelhead as soon as the customer places the order. Unless that business is a grocery store, this is simply is not going to happen. When setting up the payment policy aka credit terms, the task cannot be approached with the 100 percent cash on the barrelhead notion. A company who sets up their credit terms in a manner in which demands they are paid as a grocery store is, then they will most likely not earn any new business and will likely lose a lot of their current business. Credit terms must be set up realistically for the type of business genre it is in. In different types of industry, customers vary in what they will and will not find acceptable. For example, fresh fruit produce delivery is usually on a weekly basis if not more often, usually these types of credit terms are net 15 or net 20 at the most. A government contracted construction company, on the other hand cannot under any circumstances operate on even net 30 much less net 15 because they are paid net 90 by the government, therefore the terms they will need will be the same, net 90 or in some cases perhaps net 60 under continuous progress payment long term project accounts.

Regardless of whatever type of credit terms work for whatever type of industry any business is in, all businesses should get something in writing from the customer that spells out the terms of agreement in sale; whether that is best accomplished with estimates, purchase orders, account agreements or simply letters of confirmation, it should always be in writing.

What is obtained in writing should be simple and concise, therefore it should contain:

- What The Vendor Is Promising To Do
- When The Vendor IsPromising To Do It
- What The Customer Agrees To Pay
- Who Within The Customer's Company Will Be Responsible For Ensuring Payment Is Complete
- When The Customer Will Pay
- What The Vendor's Rights Are If The Customer Does Not Pay Or Pays Late

The goal of any set credit term is to force the customer to make a commitment to the order and protect the vendor's bottom line.

There is no black and white formula to setting up credit terms. One key aspect needed to be aware of beforehand is to set the credit terms is that are needed with respect to how the competition operates. Credit terms should be set with the knowledge of what industry standards are. This is not to say that any vendor needs to duplicate industry standards when setting up terms.

However, vendors do need to be aware of what the other companies are doing so that they can establish a credit policy that is not only effective to reducing the bad debt but is competitive and attractive to the customer when they are comparing competitors, in order to draw in new business. Often, vendors hesitate to do this research into their competitor's terms and policies, as well as their prices for that matter, but know that any potential customers will. Therefore it is imperative that a vendor know before the customer does, how they will rate.

What is often misunderstood in business is that the long-term relationships with customers are actually established by the credit and collections department.

Any company might have an outstanding sales team who has worked hard to gain the confidence and then the account of that much-wanted customer; but the very last person in the corporation that they talk to regarding that entire transaction will be the accounts receivable department. It is very important that all companies make their accounts receivable people understand this.

Accounts receivable personnel too must work just as hard to build that relationship with the customer in a positive way. They cannot remove from the company any potential of profit by extending the wrong type communications to the customers. The receivables team must also have a sales oriented mindset when collecting the bill that matches the sales team. That needs repeating: the bill collectors must approach the tasks and routines of their jobs with a sales and customer service oriented mindset. For this very reason, some companies will require the sales person to do their own collections. While on the surface, this may seem like a good idea because it holds accountability to that salesperson for what type of accounts they set up and in doing their own collections, they can soften the blow as to not upset future sales. None-the-less, this is not recommended. The sales team needs to be removed from the responsibility of setting up credit and doing collections for their accounts. It is obvious why it is not advisable to have the sales representatives determining the credit limits for their own accounts, they would sell the moon, repeatedly. However, why should the sales team not do the collections? Because, the customer needs a representative from the vendor who is 'on their side'; the salesperson needs to be the voice for the customer. No matter how wonderful and honey-sweet the collectors are, the customer still need to feel they have an "inside agent" in within the vendor company who looks out for their interests.

With the strong relationships the salespeople have already built, what is the credit-policy about? The credit policy if the final piece to the puzzle that determines the demand level for the company's product or service – sales price, product or service quality, advertising & finally the credit policy. Those are all the key pieces to the demand and supply puzzle.

The key pieces to the credit policy puzzle, in turn, are:

- Credit Standards
- Terms of Credit
- Collection Policy

Credit standards are the financial strength and creditworthiness as well as the value the vendor is to the customer that the customer must provide before being granted credit.

Terms of credit are the literal conditions of exchange. The vendor gives the customer the product or service in exchange for the customer giving the vendor asset to be known of when, where and how.

Value Based Management For Accounts Receivable

The collection policy is a very strong and important piece. The collection policy put in place determines how the customer is treated when the terms of credit are breached; and that determines if they will buy again.

Put in writing all credit policies and procedures. This policy should clearly outline the extent to which the company is willing to accept credit risk. It should clearly outline the types of credit the company is willing to extend and to which types of customers. The policy will clearly outline who has the authority to approve, deny or change credit terms and under what conditions and respective authorities. The policy will establish specified limits as to the exposure of credit and cash flow risk the company is willing to take. It should clearly define measurable benchmarks and accountabilities. Additionally, of course, the credit policy will clearly outline the systematic procedures and policies in which the credit department will conduct its daily proceedings. The credit policy shall cover the entire credit cycle, beginning from account set up and sales to accounts receivable, billing, collections and final payment posting on up to dealing with customer credits.

What To Do When The Customer Dictates Their Own Credit Terms

The type of credit policy a company is allowed to establish is limitless. Remember that a credit policy is the first line of defense against bad debt and without it even the best accounts receivable clerks in the world will not be able to collect unpaid bills. Therefor, set the credit policies with the tightest most structured limitations to ensure that the accounts receivable clerks have nothing to do when it comes to making collection calls.

With that having been said, it will still be the case that upon occasion a prospective new client will walk through the front door, ask for a credit account and then dictate to the vendor how their credit terms will set up. The vendor might have net 30 terms but the prospective new client instructs that they only pay at net 60. The vendor might have a 5% service charge for late payments but the prospective new client instructs that they do not pay service charges. The vendor might have interest rates set in place at 4.09% but the prospective new client instructs they do not pay interest rates above 1.03%. What is advised to do in this case? Should the vendor tell the potential new customer to find another supplier? Should the vendor tell the potential new customer that unless they accept the vendor's established credit terms the customer can take their business elsewhere? No, that is not what is advised. That would be a mistake.

In today's economy, a client is sometimes hard to come by and as good as diamonds or gold. Even in a good economy, that is still true. It is in any business' best interest to accept this prospective client and accept their terms. Why would this be so? For several reasons: first of all, simply because a customer is a customer and the vendor is in business to make money so the customer should not be turned away, and second of all, just because the vendor is to accept their credit terms does not mean the vendor has to increase their risk. There are little tricks vendor can do when setting up this new customer under their terms and still protect exposure to risk of receivables loss.

The vendor's terms are net 30 and the new customer insists that they will only pay on net 60 terms. The reason for this is the customer wants to await payment from their customers before paying the vendor. They bill on net 30 so they pay on net 60. What is advised in this situation is to get the principals of the business to sign an agreement that they personally guarantee that payment will be received within those 60 days and not a day later, require a personal guarantee from the high executives. A personal guarantee will affect that individual's personal credit score if the bill is late; make them aware of this. The other added benefit is that with a personal guarantee they can legally go after the individual who signed the guarantee in addition to the company.

Another trick to handling the net 60 customer is to increase the profit margin on this customer. Raise the price on this customer who insist on net 60 terms, this will reduce the cash flow risk by increasing profits.

TIP: When there is a net 60 customer account set up and traditional billings require net 30, call that customer at 50 days to ensure the bill has been entered into the payables system and will be mailed within 5 days. If not, put them immediately on credit hold and contact the person who signed the personal guarantee.

Another thing the perspective new client has instructed is that they do not pay service charges or late fees. Late fees and service charges are a wise move and it is highly recommended that they are put into place. Such fees are unrealized income and 100% pure profit. They help offset the losses of those customers who do not pay. However, this prospective new client will not pay them. Accept this condition. Why is that? That is because the company will recoup those fees elsewhere. Here again there is the option of raising the pricing structure on this client to cover the cost of late bills in lieu of service charges. It can also be done to add other fees to this customer such as delivery or fuel charges or administration fees. Whatever conditions are set to recoup the unpaid late fees and service charges, do not simply waive the service or late fees good- bye, make sure to recover those monies in other ways.

Likewise, the vendor has a policy which dictates interest rate is 4.09% but the prospective new client will not pay above 1.03%. Again, accept these terms. In doing so, change the frequency of the interest charge, such as when the company charges 4.09% interest to their other customers monthly, the business will charge 1.03% to this new perspective client daily. It can also be done to increase the base price of the costs or add non-interest bearing fees to their bill to cover the loss of the uncharged interest.

The bottom line is, be flexible. Understand that each customer is unique and therefore should be treated uniquely. Even in doing so, protect the bottom line.

If each customer is treated uniquely when setting up credit accounts, then the vendor's receivable risk will be better off.

It is very important to pay attention to how the terms of credit are set up. It is just as important that once the accounts have been set up that they are not forget about, but instead continue to monitor and adjust the account's credit terms according to how well they are paying. If a DSO is desired to be less than 30 days, then credit must be a number one priority.

Individual vs. Business Credit Applications

In setting up a company's credit policy, be aware of the mistake of commonality. The mistake of commonality is creating one set of standards and treating all the same. For example, it is the case that most companies have one credit application. They give it to a large global corporation and they give it to John Smith, private resident and small business owner. That is the mistake of commonality. The information needed from John Smith is not the same as the information needed from that global corporation.

Value Based Management For Accounts Receivable

Have at the very least two credit applications, one for larger business accounts and one for personal accounts and small businesses

The information needed from private individuals and small businesses:

- Name
- Address
- Phone
- Email address
- Social security number
- Place of employment
- Household income
- If residence is owned or rented (this presents a picture of stability vs. mobility)
- Place of previous residence
- Nearest relative not living with them
- There may be more info the business needs from the individual depending on their type of business, such as insurance or drivers license number.

The information needed from a business:

- Corporate name
- Parent company
- Type of business (LLC, Inc etc)
- Names locations of subsidiaries
- President, coo, owner or other principals name and contact info
- Accounts payable contact info
- Duns number
- How long in business

- Billing requirements
- Tax id number
- Tax exemption status
- Billing and delivery address

The application will need to have a place for a signature, which will authorize credit investigation into their credit background and will be a signature to the disclaimer, which will detail late payment fees, interest and other necessary information. It will also be their agreement for guarantee of payment.

The Three C's of Credit are Character, Collateral and Cash Flow.

Throw the first one out. Character is useless when dealing with companies. This is not a piece of advise that will be heard too often. However, whose character is going to be taken into account? Will it be the company as a whole? The accounts payable clerk dealt with whom truly has a say so over when the bills are to be paid? Will it be the board of directors? Years ago, character had its place but no more. The world is much too big. Even if the character of a company is taken into consideration as a whole, this is dangerous because there is no real method of evaluating and measuring such a thing.

By throwing character as a credit tool out of the window, that means that credit will no longer be extended based on reputation alone. This had its place once when the world was more ethically and morally motivated; but it is not this way any longer. To give an example, back in the 1950s a store would take a customer's personal check based on character alone. If the store clerk knew the customer, then the clerk assumed it was okay to take the check. Today, businesses are moving away from accepting checks all together because they are too much of a risk. A business' character is the same thing. There was a time when being a large well-known company could open an account with just about any vendor and expect to receive the highest credit terms simply because they were large and well known. That type of name recognition does not hold water any longer because everyone knows just because the company is large and world famous does not mean they are a good credit risk. This is especially true in today's day and age with large corporate government sponsored bailouts. Be careful.

In today's business world, character is no longer reliable.

Certain types of business industry require collateral to be dealt with in an exchange. Certain types of business industry do not require collateral traditionally. Under common terms, collateral is not usually a part of extending lines of credit. Even still, a company's billings may allow a security backing in the goods or services the company has furnished. States allow for liens on products or property for this purpose. Using collateral will greatly reduce the risk taken in extending credit. Whenever possible and applicable, use liens and UCC filings.

Collateral can be paramount.

With or without collateral, a customer's cash flow is what determines how they will pay their bills. For this reason, look into their financial statements to determine the cash readiness the applicant has. The type of business they deal in will also determine their cash flow. Inexperienced credit managers do not pay attention to industry type. All too often, a company extends credit based on a credit score alone without examining the deeper, financial health of the company and industry they are dealing with.

For example, Company C has recently won the bid for a very profitable, five year government contract and went to the Vendor V Company and applied for an open credit account to get supplies for this new contract. Vendor V runs the background checks and the credit checks on Company C and find they have a credit rating of eight. Sounds good, which coupled with the new government contract, will compel Vendor V to give Company C a high credit standing. The business certainly does want this company as a client but are they really worthy of the highest credit limit? Take into consideration that their new large client is now the government; it is a sure thing, right? Wrong. The government does not pay well. They pay very slow and way outside of terms; the business cannot motivate them to pay on time. Therefore, that means the company who just won this big government contract is going to be using their funds and resources on their new government contract, but they will be months upon months in the wait before they are paid back. How does that affect Vendor V? This is where cash flow becomes important. Does Company C have enough of a cash flow that will enable them to pay Vendor V's bills on time even when the government has not paid them? The credit rating alone will not indicate this. Only by examining their financial health of Company C can it be determined. It is imperative that Company C has adequate cash flow to pay the vendor's bills on time regardless of their own DSO.

Cash flow is very important; give it equal credence if not higher credence to the credit rating.

To do this, ask the customer for a financial statement; this should include the cash flow statement, balance sheet and income statement.

First, look at the cash flow statement. It should have three main parts, which are operations, investing and finance.

Start with the operations section. This section shows how much cash their company product generates. The investing section shows how much cash the company generates with investing and the finance section should outline the companies stocks and bonds they have issued. Generally, the statement of cash flows will show how the company's operations have affected its cash position by examining how the company uses its cash. The questions that the statement of cash flows answers are, *is the company generating enough cash to continue to purchase (and therefore pay) for future assets and liabilities? Does it have enough liquefiable cash to repay debt as well as buy new materials for operations?*

Second, look at the income statement; this is also called the P & L or profit and loss statement. It represents the company's health over a certain timeframe, or more specifically, what revenues were generated during this time frame and what liabilities and expenses were accrued in order to generate this revenue.

Finally, but most importantly, examine the balance sheet. The Balance sheet represents a picture of the company's financial health at any given point. It shows what the firm's assets are and how those assets are financed, whether through debt or equity.

When looking at the balance sheet, remember these equations:

Total Assets = Total Liabilities + Total Equity

Net Working Capital = Current Assets – Current Liabilities

Owner's Equity = Net Worth = Total Assets – Total Liabilities

Professional Services & Credit

It is common for a professional service, such as a small doctor's office or a private music instructor to avoid running credit reports or asking for financials.

While it is uncommon, it is not necessary for a service provider to forgo the credit background check. In cases such as these, professional services should collect information from the prospective customer that will aid in the collection of fees not otherwise covered by insurance or other service payment means.

Professional services will offer to the prospective new client a client data form that will obtain the same information as a standard credit application. This form will obtain the standard information of client name, address, age, phone, place of employment and the like but it will include asking for their social security number and alternative forms of contact including nearest relative not living with them. It should also request bank information along with standard insurance information when applicable to the type of professional service. Repeat the questions, applying them to the spouse or responsible party. Do not be afraid to ask for as much information as deemed necessary in order to reduce risk. People are used to these sorts of things and quite expect it.

Most professional offices, for example a doctor's office, will require co-payment in advance. This standard practice is for obvious reasons a very good idea. However, it does not guarantee client out of pocket costs have been covered. The insurance company, for example, may reject part of the claim. Depending on the deductible, there may be additional billings to the client. Will they pay? That is determined by running a credit report.

Value Based Management For Accounts Receivable

Unpaid medical bills account for the vast majority of past due consumer debts reported to the credit bureaus by collection agencies; often times the rest of the applicant's credit report will show good payments to their creditors, but they will still have unpaid medical bills that have been reported to a collection agency.

On the Customer Data Form, it will require a signature from the client that mandates their agreement to paying by the company's terms and that they accept full responsibility for the portions not covered by insurance and giving their consent to a credit bureau report ran on them.

When a payment plan is agreed upon by the consumer, do not rely on them to make their payments on their own, obtain their bank account routing and account numbers and their authorization for auto draft payments. Much of the time, it isn't a matter of no funds that prevent clients from paying for their professional services such as their doctors, it is more the case of the client not wanting to allocate payment to these professional services because they'd rather spend the money elsewhere and sometimes, the consumer just forgets because it is not a normal bill to them.

This might seem like a novel idea, a doctor's practice running a credit report, but it is also a good idea. It will give an idea of the new client's ability to pay and it will show in advance of billing what is needed to do in order to reduce the risk.

Value Based Management For Accounts Receivable

A Credit Horror Story

In a medium sized, middle class, mid-western town there is a family owned audio and video installation company. This company has existed for three generations; the grandchildren of the founder are now running the shop. During the term of the original owner, the business started out small and struggling like any new business. During the term of the second generation, the parents of the current owners, the business grew very well and prospered financially. The business is now over 60 years old and idealistic, young and brilliant grandchildren now run the company. Both of the current owners are intelligent, career minded, college graduates whom, before taking over the family business, worked executive positions in corporate America, one in the technology industry and one in the financial industry. Their backgrounds were well suited for running the family business.

Like anybody in corporate America, they had the typical gripes and complaints that we all do, working 8:00 to 5:00 in the office. So when the opportunity came for them to own and run the family business, they were ecstatic. Now they could come and go as they pleased, make all the decisions on their own, decide what is what and feel the true freedom of business ownership. The first thing they did when they started running the business was to remove the dress code. The company had a business attire dress code for the office workers and uniforms for the service crew. The new bosses, tired of the suits they had worn for years, started coming to work in jeans and t-shirts, even shorts and allowed their employees to do the same. The formal uniforms of the service crew were replaced by company logo t-shirts they wore with their own jeans or shorts and comfortable athletic shoes.

The second thing they did was to spend large amounts of company savings in remodeling the interior of the outdated and well-worn offices. Interior office walls were re-arranged and created and all employees were given their own new, four-walled with a window, private office. The cubicles and open desks were gone. Even the filing clerk had an office.

The next few decisions they made were along the same lines of relaxing the atmosphere in an effort to make the place, what they considered to be, an enjoyable work place. That was valuable to them and it all cost them a large amount of their reserve cash, reducing liquid assets considerably. Later, as it will seen, this reduction almost ended their business.

Now with everything in place as they wanted it, they spent their first few months enjoying their newfound freedom as business owners. They would come in late in the morning or early afternoon, leave early, not show up at all some days. As time went on, the business began to pull them into the groove of the work-a-day week and the new owners began spending their time, resources and energy into trying to discover new technology to bring into the company and new directions in which to expand.

The employees that they inherited, for the most part, worked at the company for ten, twenty, even thirty or more years. They knew their jobs and they knew their routine. There was no need for the new owners to teach these employees their jobs; what they failed to do however, was to learn these jobs themselves. They trusted their employees to carry on, business as usual.

Sales became a concentrating force in the new owners; they wanted to boost revenue by increasing their customer base and growing geographically with regional large companies whose potential receivables were extremely high.

What these larger companies, the big fish, were offered was service in the old fashioned style of sixty years ago. The products themselves were basically the same things any other company would install and at comparable prices. What did it, was the service – outstanding customer service. Outstanding customer service is a powerful tool and it is a key tool in using the Value Bases Approach To Credit & Collections Management.

When these new fish started taking the bait, the new owners were again, ecstatic. They envisioned all the money that would come in from these new, large customers.

Within the audio and visual industry, there is plenty of room for repeat business. There is service, maintenance, upgrades and repairs that will always need done. The prime revenue base of this company before the big sales boom consisted of mainly repeat business and a small amount of new customers, small to medium sized businesses from word-of-mouth advertising. There really was not any real sales force and therefore there really was not any real credit and collections policy in place. The existing customers were long-term customers who paid their bills because they had for years.

When the first and second generations ran the company, when a new customer wanted to make a purchase, an immediate down payment was required that equated the company's cost in the project, so right up front, all costs were covered to the break-even point. For the remaining portion, the pure profit portion of the balance due, a credit bureau report was ran on the new customer, if they had good credit they were allowed net 15 terms and installation began immediately. If the customer's credit score was not good, they were still allowed net 15 terms, but installation was not started until the full balance was paid. If the customer asked, payment plans were allowed. This was the policy put into place years ago and it had remained that way from the very beginning. There were often many new jobs on the books not began because the company was waiting for payment in full on the amounts due. In truth, if a company could not pay up front, there was no sale. Remember that credit is a choice, and companies do not have to offer credit terms if they do not want to.

The new owners considered this policy jeopardizing to the new sales efforts, especially at the dollar volume they were going for. In today's day and age, customers are used to net 30 terms and being billed for the amount due after the completion of the job and it has been accepted as a job well done. Therefore, in this, the new owners were right. If they wanted to push sales, then they needed to revamp the credit policy.

Unfortunately, neither of the new owners running the place had any experience with credit or collections and so their focus was on sales. They went after big million dollar corporations, federal and state contracts worth similar dollars, the big fish. Fish who, in all reality, were big enough that they would have a credit application already made that would dictate their expected credit terms.

The new owners accepted these credit terms, never questioning anything. They never ran credit reports because in their reasoning, these companies were so large and so rich, the cost of running a credit report was mute. They never set credit limits on any of these new customers. They gave them net 30 terms and a lot of them were given net 60 at the customer's request and in some cases even net 90 terms.

Not one dime of the job was invoiced until after installation, after the new owners talked to the customer personally and found out if they were satisfied. This is great customer service, however it entailed making calls, leaving messages, receiving messages, returning message, and playing telephone tag. Consequently, it would be well past a month after job completion before any invoice was created; with net 60 terms, the billing was not even due for at least

90 days past job completion. What's more, no down payments were ever asked for out of fear of upsetting the new customer.

As this first chapter has explained, just because a company is well known or has the cash flow, does not mean they are going to pay all their invoices on time. It is a matter of value and timing and need.

Much to the shock and dismay of the new owners, their receivables began to look very, very bad. They had hundreds of thousands of dollars over six months past due and in some cases, even up to a year past due. What did they do about it? They hired a collections clerk.

The new collections clerk was set up in her office and given the receivables books and told to make collections calls, and she did. The result of which was that most of these past due customers had their past due accounts shut down, no new installations and no repairs (except that which was covered by contracted warranties or issues do to faulty product or installation).

Consequently, there was no longer good word-of-mouth advertising being extended.

With the cost of the unpaid jobs cutting into the cash flow of the business, new sales came to a halt. Recall the large amounts of cash spent on remodeling the offices and other monies spent? This is where those financial decisions began to have a detrimental affect.

The company was losing money fast, and spiraling downward.

What was needed and therefore created was a sound credit policy. This credit policy extended credit to technology oriented companies who utilized technology in their daily business practices as a main focal point. The credit policy limited credit to those customers who only used technology as a tool to conduct their regular mode of business, which focused on something else entirely. This credit policy required down payments and in some cases, progress payments as the job continued. Every customer had a credit limit. The credit policy also took into account the flow of dollars from each customer; for example, if a customer was sending in steady stream of cash and their account was profitable, despite the aging, sales and service continued.

It was also important to focus on the unresolved, past due balances. Any good credit and collections professional will tell state that the time-value of money is imperative. The longer unpaid invoices sit on the books, the more it costs the company. Therefore, the unpaid balances were put into two groups, one who still represented a profit and the other did not. On the ones that still represented a profit, it was arranged for discounts on balances due and amortized monthly payment terms, service-oriented incentives were offered for payments received and time was spent with each customer building a relationship with them on behalf of the company. Over time, the effort worked and that group of invoices was paid. For the other stack, a repossession company was hired to repossess the equipment. They successfully repossessed most of all the equipment. The rest was written off.

The most important thing was that the company could resume their hard-hitting sales efforts, and by following the credit policy put into place, their receivables would prosper profitably.

The moral of the story here is that yes, being able to add new customers to the books is very good for business; however, new customers mean nothing until these new customer pay their bills. A perceptive sales force is one who is credit and collections savvy as well.

Research the credit worthiness of each new prospective client before extending him or her credit; Dun & Bradstreet is an excellent credit reference tool and highly recommended for this purpose.

CHAPTER TWO – Policies & Procedures

Developing The Credit Policy

In order to write a credit policy, six questions must be answered:

- What is the company mission?
- What are the company's goals?
- Who has specific credit responsibilities and authorities?
- How is credit evaluated?
- How are collections handled?
- What are the company's terms of sale?

Credit policies are something that will need continual attention. Credit policies are not just something that are set up then forgotten about. It is advisable to review credit policies quarterly, if not at the very least twice per year. In the same manner that it is needed to review the individual credit limits on the individual customer accounts every so often, it is also needed to review the company's basic credit policy and do not hesitate to make adjustments and changes. As a business grows and develops its niche in the business world, the operators of the business will find that the credit needs of the customers will begin to become more funneled. By that, it is meant that within the business' particular industry, there will be nuances that are unique to that industry and consequently those nuances will translate into variable needs of credit to the customers. Nuances can be good but they can also be dangerous; be aware and adjust accordingly. The bottom line is to look at the DSO and compare it to the receivables profitability, how is it performing? Examine the accounts that are creating a high DSO and compare them to the accounts that are low DSOs, which are creating a higher profit margin, where are the holes in the credit policy? Keep the profit margin in mind, it is not solely about the aging.

The aspects of credit and collections are not an exact science; they are an art form to be nurtured along gracefully over time. There will be trial and error along with the growth and learned experiences.

As an example to emphasize, a businessperson retired from the city and bought a farm out in the country. He began operating a farm equipment rental business out of his personal farm/residence during his retirement. Right away, he advertised the popular "No Money Down! Six Months Same As Cash!" The retired businessperson got the business! He certainly did. That no money down and six months same as cash appealed to many people. That type of credit does appeal to people but it does not appeal to the right type of customer, not with adequate cash flow to pay their liabilities. It is not preferable to open a credit account for someone who cannot get credit except under special circumstances. Yes, a lot of businesses will be generated from this type of credit policy; but the type of businesses that do this type of thing also take large hits on their DSOs and they operate their profit margin on a volume basis, and more than likely they can afford to do that. Nevertheless, a start-up company and most direct sales and service companies cannot. This is a policy intended to increase business sales by motivating buyers currently lacking in adequate cash to make an immediate purchase. Sometimes the company will see this called 'dating' in the business world. What this means is that businesses will 'date' the invoice up to six months after the sale and shipment of goods. This might be of value when a business is over run by inventory or they are a seasonal business and want to spread their receivables out to the off-season. This method of credit can be of use, in limited situations, but in most situations it is not advisable.

Credit Policies

Even though the first step in determining what is needed to put into place for the company's credit policy will be to research industry standards and competitor policies, it is not desired to simply copy what the research has uncovered. Set up a credit policy that works on the unique level of the company.

Make sure the newly created credit policy takes into account the company's cash flow needs. The policy will make sure that there is enough cash flow to operate the business and pay the company's own bills on time.

The first rule is simply and straight forward - *do unto others as you would have them do unto you*; in other words, before any expectations can be made towards having a positive receivables balance, the company must pay its own bills on time.

Once the company's payables policy reflects no less than what is expected from the customers, only then is it acceptable to begin focusing on the receivables policy.

Once the work on the company's receivables policies begins, start by putting the company's credit policy down on paper but do not etch it into stone. Remember it needs to stay flexible from client to client and year to year. A credit policy will be in place and it will guide the company through outstanding receivables but it also needs to stay flexible to account for any situation and circumstance that will come along. A good and effective credit policy is one that will be developed over the years. For this reason, it is necessary to review the credit policy every period to make sure it is still meeting the company's needs.

Not only is it necessary to review the credit policy from time to time but it is also necessary to review each account's credit terms periodically to make sure they are at the level they need to be set. It may be necessary to increase someone's limit that is paying well and buying a lot. Likewise, it may be necessary to reduce the limit or even put on credit hold someone who is not paying well. If the latter is an action to take on an account, ensure that the account is not producing a profit, do not cut off revenue despite aging.

Continual monitoring is the key to knowing what to do when.

Setting Up Procedures

Make sure employees know why they are asked to do the things they do. More often than not, a new employee will have been hired who optimizes payroll savings; which usually means they are qualified but not overly so. When they step in on the first day, they have the knowledge familiarity but they will need to go through training to learn how the company does things. The person who does the training is another associate on the same level. The person training them knows how to do the job, step-by-step, and they teach the new employee in this manner. The new person learns the procedures in this way. For the first few weeks, or first couple of months, they are concentrating on learning the steps to their job. The questions they ask reflect feedback in how they are performing task-wise. Once they learn the task and grow comfortable with them, they become great employees who come to work and do their job well - as long as things remain routine. When things become unique, it throws them off and a myriad of questions and problems occur. Why is this? It is because that employee knows how to do the procedures of their job but they do not know why they do them. Most likely they have spent most of their career doing the same type of work, but have not learned other departments and other functions and so they cannot make the connection between what they do and what others do. It is very critical that they know this.

For example, does the purchasing clerk know why they put the yellow copy of the purchase order in File Y and the pink copy in Basket X? Do they understand that the pink copy is picked out of Basket X and matched to the shipping manifest so that accounts payable can verify what was ordered against what was received before paying the bill? Do the receiving personnel understand that the slash marks they make on the shipping manifest are tallies that are used in the inventory control report to the CFO? Does each employee understand the very important reasons that they are asked to perform each job task in the specific way they are asked to do so? It is imperative that they do.

If each employee in the organization does not have a clear understanding of what happens before them and what happens after them as well as have a clear understanding of the overall entire process flow of the company then what exists employed are not value based employees but non-value based task parrots. Employees who have a clear understanding of how what they do affects the rest of the company as well as the bottom line, make fewer mistakes and are more proactive in problem prevention and process improvement.

These are important things to consider. When considering the development and improvement of accounts receivable, things of this nature are not added to the list of considerations. It is not regarded that the understanding and knowledge of the purchasing clerk affects the aging and profitability of the receivables report. This is the butterfly affect.

This is why cross training is very important. Not only does it provide the company with resources for job coverage when employees are missing but it improves the intelligence with which the company operates and that improves the bottom line, the receivables. Do not just teach the employees how to do their job in a task oriented method; teach them why they do those things, how it affects the next person, and how what they do looks in the books and reports. This gives them a sense of importance and understanding that will improve their contribution to the company.

Knowledge is power and power converts into profits and the best companies share knowledge openly and proactively.

Google Maps

One small trick that can be applied to the credit evaluations process is the use of Google Maps street view. It is expected that the company already verifies the address and phone numbers on the credit applications, for both consumer and business applicants, but take it a step further and also look at the property in question using Google Maps street view. (Be aware that the addresses in Google can sometimes be approximate and not exact locations.)

The reason for this is to verify what has been asserted in the application. For example, an application was once received for credit from a farming business and it was accompanied by a farmer's agricultural tax exemption certificate. When the address was pulled up in Google Maps, it was a used car sales lot. When the phone number was called on the application, it was questioned why the address appeared to go to a car lot when the application said it was a farm. It was explained that the farmer who applied for credit also owned the car lot. However, the farm was at a very different location. What the applicant was attempting to do was to obtain supplies for his car lot without having to pay taxes for these supplies. He knew that they would check out the validity of the farm being in business but he did not expect them to use Google Maps to look at the property.

To give another example of when Google Maps came in handy, this customer had ordered very large supplies. Using Google Maps, it was revealed that the business was in a very tight place and there was no way to get the large delivery truck around the back, as was going to be needed. This was useful to know ahead of time.

Another example of when Google Maps came in handy was in the processing of a consumer application. This applicant applied for a low income discount for certain products and was having them shipped to his home. His million-dollar home, as Google Maps revealed. Further investigation into the matter did reveal that the applicant was trying to apply for benefits for which he did not qualify. Google Maps was very useful in discovering this.

It is imperative that caution be exercised fully in the use and application of Google maps images. Under no circumstances should it be allowed to be used for discriminatory purposes or biased judgements.

One example that can be offered in which the image returned in Google maps almost led to bias is when a particular consumer ordered high dollar technology to be shipped to his home, applying for net-30 store credit as payment. Google images verified the home as a residence, everything that the application asserted. However, Google images revealed that the residential home was very low income and in a very low income and high crime neighborhood. The very first thought that came was that this invoice would not be paid on time. However, nothing other than the image revealed failed the credit and background check. The items were shipped. The items were paid in full and on time.

Credit management is not a science, it is an art form that only time and experience can improve.

Limiting Empowerment In Making Credit Decisions

Credit decisions are a learned art form. All the programs, software and formulas and all the other tools in the world can be utilized in credit management, but in the end, credit management is truly an art form. Exactly what is meant by a learned art form is that it takes education, knowledge, and financial experience to make the right credit decisions but it takes experience the company can only grow over time. Not only that, but the real issue is that two people can and often make different credit decisions, that is ok for the most part but the company's needs consistency among the accounts.

Too many chefs spoil the soup and too many credit-empowered employees spoil the accounts. The DSO is controlled by the credit risks the company has set up on the account, the tighter the control of risk the better the accounts will do. If the company has too many people authorized to make credit decisions the tightness of the control will loosen.

Empowerment can be a good thing. However, too much of it can hurt the business. For example, there is a large global company that has fifty credit analysts. Each credit analyst had a territory assigned to them based on geography and they handled all the credit decisions within that territory. The result of that is that there are fifty individual little companies doing things their own way and no two the same way. If a sales clerk could not get the credit limit he wanted for his new client, then he simply called another credit analyst and bingo, he got what he wanted. Every day, any client's account would have his limit raised then lowered then raised again, determined by whatever the immediate need was. Eventually, this company saw the error of this and restricted the empowerment down to a manageable level. The credit analysts were not happy because it turned them from analysts to clerks. Even still, they saw their profits rise in the next quarter simply because they now had the one thing they lacked before: universal accountability and consistency.

Removing empowerment and installing accountability and consistency is essential.

Regardless of the size of the company or the number of people in the accounts receivable department, there is the need to restrict the empowerment to make decisions down to as few as possible. Then those people are to be held entirely accountable for the DSO.

One of the key players in any business is the Credit/Collections Manager. That person needs to be held solely and entirely responsible for the DSO – bottom line. The Credit Manager will be responsible for everything that has to do with the company being paid from the first contact a sales clerk makes to a prospective new client to the collector trying to collect a past due bill. For this reason, the sales team as well as the entire accounts receivable team will report to the Credit Manager. The viability of having the sales team answer to the credit manager is not precedent but it is profitable. The appropriate person for this job is a manager who is both credit savvy and sales savvy, and equally so.

Depending on the size of the company, it may be possible to restrict all credit limits and order approval decisions to the credit manager. Alternatively, the business may be too large and the credit manager may have to have assistant credit managers or professional credit analysts to help him or her with this task. Either way, limit the empowerment to as few as possible.

One valuable notion to take away from this book is the knowledge that credit and collections, accounts receivable, is not an exact science, it is an art form. If it was an exact science, the company's managers could teach the formula to their employees and rest assured that every decision made on every account is the exact same one that the manager would make and that it is the right one. However, it does not work that way. Go apply for a personal loan at three different places and what will occur are three different quotes even though all three places will see the same credit scores. The reason for this is that everyone interprets the data they see in front of them differently, depending on their own experiences. One good example of this is a personal credit score that ranges from 600 to 640; in general, personal credit scores above 700 are good, ones above 800 are excellent and ones below 599 are poor. Credit scores in the 600s are harder to gauge, especially ones in the lower 600s. It is possible for a couple who has a credit score of 625 to receive at one bank a thirty-thousand dollar auto loan and at another bank be turned down flat. That is a very big difference in offers, but it is a very good example of how the employees will interpret things differently, one from the other. So what is to be done about that? What is to be done is to review the credit policy often, the credit limits of the accounts continually and over time, be able to see trends and train the employees with what the expectations are.

Managing The Payables

"Physician heal thyself." No truer words could be spoken about managing a company's credit and collections department. Unless the company's payables are current and in good standing, there is no way it will be able to manage the receivables with any effectiveness. There was a situation once whereas a company, Company A, withheld payment to a vendor, Vendor B, because that vendor owed the company twice as much - past due. What was done was to reduce the amount due by Vendor B by the amount the company, Company A owed and to re-mail an updated invoice to Vendor B. It was not very long after that the vendor called to collect on the amount owed them. It was explained to the vendor how the amount the company owed was used to reduce the amount the vendor owed. However, the vendor representative calling insisted on full payment instead. It was told to her that payment could be sent out; however, their bill with the company was now at age forty days. The vendor was asked to pay in full. There was dead air on the line. She had absolutely no clue her company owed the money. Apparently, she was so focused on collecting that she did not really hear what was said about the offsetting of their balance due. After comprehending, she accepted the deal and while the books would balance, overall she was not going to be able to show actual cash received for this against her DSO.

It cannot be stressed enough how important it is the company pays their own bills on-time. It is a small world and the company's past due bills within its own region, within its own industry will be known to others.

When the receivables clerk calls to collect a bill and is given the same excuse the payables clerk just used on someone else, is the company in a good position? No, the company's position and integrity is compromised.

Use offsetting for those accounts that are both customer and vendor. This is a common practice and will be almost expected (when the other person is aware of it that is). If this cannot be done, volunteer a payment plan so that the debt obligations are being met.

Charging Interest And/Or Finance Charges

Most small to medium sized businesses are afraid to charge interest or late fees to customer's invoices that are past due. This is quite understandable, customer service is always the number one factor to any business and the last thing desired is to do is upset the customer. However, will it really upset them if interest or late fees are charged? Think about it this way, every single day that the invoice is late is costing money. Not charging the customer interest or late fees is the same as giving them an interest free loan. No bank in this world would ever extend an interest free loan, so why should a company that is in business to make money? As long as the fees and interest policies are dealing with the customer fairly, they expect the business to recoup its losses. Check around for what is normal in the industry.

Apply Credits Or No

The longer a business has a relationship with their customer the more likely it will be that their books will have some credits. Are the credits to be applied or not? Half the customers will expect the business to automatically apply them and half the customers will expect the business to not to apply them until they say to, and all of them will be firm in the opinion that doing it any other way but what they expect is irregular.

The options of choice are one of two things, the business can make it a policy that when credits arise the customer is called each and every time to ask if they want it applied, but that may annoy the customer and it will be tedious.

Value Based Management For Accounts Receivable

So the other option, being the most effective option, is get to know the customers and learn if they want their credits applied or not and on each account apply the ones who want them applied and don't on the ones who don't want them to be.   Doing it this way is more work than having one universal policy and expecting the customers to accept that policy. However, one condition of VBM is that the company treat each customer as an individual and deal with them in whatever manner promotes the best optimal profitability from that customer.

Keep Up With Credit Review Even On Good Customers

Especially in accounts receivable, it is one thing to collect a past due debt, but it is entirely another thing to not have debt fall past due. Receivables are an asset, but once the asset of receivables reaches a certain age unpaid, it can no longer be counted as an asset; it is then becomes a write-off and the product or service attached to that write-off was given away free.

The best accounts receivable personnel spend more time on credit management than debt collections. Any receivables department that is spending the majority of their day making collection calls is not spending enough time on credit management. Receivables departments should be spending the majority of their day on credit management to prevent the bad debt.

Every account, when the balance rises above the account's credit limit is to be immediately reviewed. Additionally, pull credit reports on the largest clients periodically and find out how they are doing. Is their financial health improving or getting worse? If it is getting worse, then lower their credit limit or at the very least, keep tight reigns on their balances in order to prevent debt loss should things snowball. The company has to keep an eye out and perceive future problems before they arise.

Estimating the probability of account default is an ongoing process, throughout the life cycle of every account. It is an ongoing thing and it must continue to be so throughout the service relationship of each customer. In a nut shell, stay on top of each accounts cash flow stability and their future ability to generate this cash flow in order to pay their bills.

In order to do this it is important to monitor commercial industry trends. For example, if the company sells to automotive manufacturers, they need to be aware of the current trends in the automotive economy. If the company sells to residential construction companies, what is the forecast for new home sales?

It cannot be stressed enough, it is simply not enough to only monitor the paid history of accounts. While that will be the strongest influence in the management of the company credit policies, it is also necessary to be aware of coming storms in the industries to which the customers apply.

Credit Reports And NACM

A subscription to a good and reliable credit-reporting agency is recommended. There are several from which to choose. Choose the one that offers the required services needed for the budget available, but make sure they are reputable and reliable. Dun & Bradstreet is one such company, a very good source.

Another useful tool is the NACM, National Association of Credit Managers. www.nacm.org. The NACM is an association formed by credit managers nationwide who offer resources and networking for credit managers in aide of making good credit decision. Becoming a member of the NACM is a good idea. The NACM provides access other credit managers with whom to network.

Checklists

Checklists are a valuable part of any business establishment. No accounting department, for example, can function without a checklist making sure all of end of quarter or end of year processing steps have been completed. Mistakes are less likely to happen if there is in place a checklist to refer.

Any accounts receivable department is no different. In fact, accounts receivable personnel, just like any standard accounting personnel, should be solely and entirely dependent on a checklists to facilitate the proper account set up, information retrieval, credit monitoring and collections processes.

Checklist for Account Set Up

When a new customer is acquired, credit terms aside, a checklist should be used to ensure all steps necessary in setting up that client have been taken. For example, have all signatures in the correct places been acquired from the customer? Are all tax forms in file from the customer? These things, while important, are easy to overlook and if they are overlooked, later on that could be detrimental.

Checklists For Information Retrieval

When pulling together all the information necessary with which to make a credit decision, a checklist can provide guidance as to what is necessary to acquire, making sure nothing is overlooked. For example, a checklist will help to instruct whether a credit report should be pulled on the local division or the parent company. Which report is needed? Who is paying the bills? What type of business entity is it? Are they a seasonal company? If any of these or other questions go unanswered, the credit decision will be faulty.

•Checklist For Collections Efforts

Expect to encounter times when it is necessary to take a customer to court in order to collect past due balances. It is important to ensure that all steps required by law have been conducted with evidence before this happens. A check list will verify that necessary legal steps have taken place. Has the customer received certified written notice? Did the notice contain all required wording and information. Was the invoice correct? Were all issues addressed? These are the types of questions that are addressed with a checklist.

When the check list is set up, it is important that certain items are included. One such item is ensuring that it has been identified exactly who is responsible for paying the bill, such as the corporate office or the branch office or the company owner. The checklist needs to ensure that all legal requirements for billing and collections have been met for both the company's and the customer's geographic regions. The checklist will also list out the timeline of expected collections and billings steps.

Changes In Credit Policies

A credit policy is one that grows and changes over time. It is not written out, etched in stone, never to be altered. As times change, companies need to change; business entities who do not evolve die out, and the credit policty of a company is not immune to this. When is it time to change the credit policy? The answer to this comes by evaluating how the proposed changes will effect the company's value. Receivables are revenue which is part of the company's value. Does the change bring in more value than it costs to make the change? Does the change bring in no additional value at all despite the additional cost? Be able to analyze the specific time value of money in within the receivables with and without the change. The point is that change is necessary, upon occasion, for a growing company.

CHAPTER THREE – All About Billings

Statements & Invoices

One of the important but most often overlooked credit policy steps is the design of statements and invoices. This is very important because it is the statements and invoices that let the customers know that it is time to pay, what to pay and how. Keep the invoices and statements clean and simple with large print and plain type. Do not use more than two colors beyond the black color of the type font and avoid as much graphics as possible. Use tear away, perforated sections that the customer can just tear and mail in a pre-addressed stamped envelope. Make it as easy for them as possible. Try to avoid putting internal-company codes and wording that the customer does not need to see. Itemize things in the descriptions of charges but keep the itemizations simple and obvious.

Things the invoices and statements will include are:

- An Invoice Number
- A Purchase Order Number
- An Order Date
- An Invoice Date
- A Due Date
- The Customer's Account Number
- The Company's Vendor Number In Their Payables System

- A Complete, Clear & Concise Description Of What They Are Being Billed For
- Itemized Pricing
- Total Amount Due
- The Company's Accounts Receivable Department Contact Phone Number, Web Address, Etc.
- A simple disclaimer giving discounts for early payment, finance charges, interest and/or late fees as would pertain to the customer.
- Customer Obligation Section: this section explains customer obligations; such as timely payments, communication when there is a problem, etc.
- A Non-Transfer Claus: This brief statement prohibits customers from transferring their account or obligations or any such relationship with the company to a third party without the company's written consent.

Invoicing

What is the number one marketing piece for any business? By the subheading of this section, it can be guessed that it is the invoice. It does not matter how much money is spent on advertising, marketing and public relations, it does not matter how many free company packs of sticky notes are given out, the number one piece of information that is constantly in front of the customer's faces are the invoicing and statements they are billed. The company's invoice and statement is the one thing they see continually. It is the company's first,second and third impression. That is one very big reason why it is necessary to ensure that every statement and invoice that is sent out is correct. That invoice is one thing that can be assured that will be read in its entirety.

They will scrutinize the invoice. Therefore, make the invoice a valuable marketing tool. Put the company slogan on it, put the current sales event on it and put the information on that invoice that is needed to promote the business.

Most companies never fully utilize the most valuable marketing piece their company has access to which is their Invoices. Of all things the company's name goes on, the invoices and statements that re sent out are the single most often read piece of material by the customers.

Getting It Right

As it is with the invoice being the most important piece of marketing the company name will be on, it can be understood that getting everything on the invoice correct is very important. There can be no mistakes on the invoices.

For example when a customer calls with an error in their billing, it can be assumed that the issue was corrected and another invoice would be sent out. No hassles. right? Wrong. What needs to be realized is that it was not that quick and simple for the customer. When they got that invoice and it did not match up to their records, their first inclination was to assume that the company billing them were the ones who were right and they tried to reconcile to that. However, they could not and by the time, they realized the bill was the one wrong and not them, they had already spent precious time on it only to end in frustration. Waiting on the corrected invoice holds up their payables.

That is the marketing that was just created for the company, one that ended in negative imagery to the customer.

Value Based Management For Accounts Receivable

Traditional business schools will teach that accounting in a company is non-value added time, much less quality control for accounting. That notion is outdated. Any activity within an organization that prevents negative campaign images and mistakes before the customer is extremely value added. Therefore, it is very necessary to concentrate on putting into place some kind of quality control for the billings.

Keep It Simple

Simplicity to the customer means efficiency and quality. Keep the invoices straight forward and as simple and clean as possible. Psychologically, complex looking invoices have the connotation of over billing; why that is so, is because to the customer they have one clean transaction. They order, they buy. They do not need to know the internal accounting codes. The more straightforward and simple, the less hassle and better.

Invoice Their Way

No matter how many customers a company has and how large that company is, each customer to that company will have unique needs. Not all accounting departments are set up the same way, just like snowflakes, no two are alike and therefore each of the customers will have unique accounting needs. The invoices sent to them need to address their individual needs. Create a way to customize invoices towards each client. This will be costly but it is very important and in the end, the benefits will outweigh the costs.

Discounts

Consider offering a discount for early payments. For example, when normal terms are net 30, then offer a 3% discount for payments received within 10 days. What discount is offered and for how early of a payment must be determined by looking at the books, but many companies look to take advantage of discounts and will pay early in order to receive the savings. This improves the DSO.

Statements

Some companies will only pay by statements, and that is ok. Therefore, the statement while being a summary of the invoices, needs to have all the same pertinent information as the invoices. The most common mistake on statements is that they do not have the details their payables department needs, such as purchase order numbers for each invoice listed on the statement, order person, job details, etc.

The most direct method for listing this information is linearly. Take a lesson from Microsoft Excel or Apple Mac Numbers; both very useful programs that have excellent layout styles for invoicing. Sometimes the most useful tools are the simplest.

How To Bill

With regards to how to bill, the most cost effective way is digitally by either email or allowing the customer to download their bills online via the company's website. Not all customers are going to be able to do this, but the numbers are growing each day so a wise company will be prepared. Some larger customers will even have their own online methods for vendors to be able to upload their bills to them and this is wonderful.

For the rest who still need paper copies, find out if they will allow faxed bills instead of mailed ones and if so set up an online e-fax account so invoices can uploaded digitally, saving cost of paper.

If none of the above will work for the last straggling customers, do add a few cents paper charge to their account.

Remember that timeliness is most important to both statements and invoices. Invoices should be mailed out immediately. Statements monthly and in some cases, quarterly statements are also a good idea. Ensure that the invoices are immediate. Ensure that the statements go out on the same day each month or quarter.

A Billing Horror Story

The end of chapter one presented a credit horror story. It is now time for a billing horror story about the same company. At this point it must be confessed that not all of the problems attributing to the severe past due aging of the company in question resulted from improper credit policies. Some of it had to do with a horrible billing process.

This is how their billings went:

Initially, the sales clerks who set up the account would have gone out to the customer's location to make the sale. For example, pretend that they were going out to a company called Consolidated Industries to sell them an entire interoffice intercom system, audio/video equipment in the board room, new phones and computer networking systems; a very large job. The sales clerks would have a report of everything the customer required to be installed, where and with what parts. Then the sales clerks would put a price on it; they would give a bid to the customer. In this scenario, the sales clerks might have quoted total cost plus labor, parts and installation at $250,000. The customer signs the agreement and the sales clerks give the order (the report) to the service manager. The service manager then looks at the report, decides how many days and how many men it will take to do the installation, book the men and days into the system and then give the report to the warehouse manager. The warehouse manager then reviews what parts are needed and inventories what is on hand. He then orders the rest. When all the parts are in, the report goes back to the service manager. The service manager then sends the crew to do the installation.

Part of the inventory needed for such things are massive amounts of wires, nuts and bolts. In a job such as this, it is almost impossible to determine beforehand how much wiring, nuts and bolts will be needed. Therefore, hordes of it are taken out to the job site and the technicians are to count how much of each are used each day and write it down on a piece of paper. Each time one of the ordered parts is installed, the technetium writes it down on the paper. Much of the time, when one specific part was ordered, it is common that it must be switched out for another similar type. For example, if speaker 3456 from Sound Corp was ordered for the boardroom, and it is determined that it will not fit in the space, the technicians will switch it for another same cost or near same cost speaker, such as 99978 from Hear Corp. When they do this, they are to write it down.

In the end what exists is a report that lists out what all the parts were supposed to be for that job accompanied by several pieces of scratch paper hand written by the technicians listing out the differences that need adjusted as well as the amount to bill for wiring and nuts and bolts. These papers will also list out how many hours they actually spent on the job, to bill for labor.

Therefore, the report and hand written papers now go to the billing clerk. She starts out by inputting the information in the report. Then she will make the adjustments that are written on the paper. The problem here is that what is turned in by the crew is literally a scrap of paper with part numbers all over it, written like a doodle pad. The billing clerk has to figure out, like a puzzle, what each number and letter on the paper was meant to represent. The paper might say JCO338, which is an input switcher; does that mean that JCO338 was used in place of the RJO339 input switcher already on the report or that it was used in addition to it? The billing clerk will have to chase down all these technicians, who are out on other jobs, to ask them and find out, or she can just make a guess.

Another problem is that the technicians, not really being the paper and pencil type, never write down everything they should and only guess at the amounts of wire, nuts, bolts and hours, usually at the end of the project.

Therefore, the billing clerk, who probably has an accounting degree, must have some sort of mechanical aptitude in order to do her accounting clerk billing job.

With all that struggling, finally the clerk has the amount to bill which in reality came out to a grand total of $275,000. But wait! Remember the quote? The sales clerk agreed in writing to $250,000 to the customer. Why the difference? In the end, labor hours were more than expected, (and usually are), not all the cost of wiring was included in the quote because it could not be determined what would be needed and the speaker and input switch trades were an upgrade. The job just cost more.

However, only $250,000 can be billed because that was the quote.

So billing clerk has to play with the numbers until the invoice matches the $250,000 quote. How does she do that? She lowers the price on parts, cuts down on labor costs, plays with the figures until the bill is $250,000. This type of billing is very inconsistent. No two jobs are ever billed with the same costing structures because the billable facts must be adjusted each and every time in order to match the quote. Obviously, what this does, consequently, is drastically reduce the profit margin of the job.

When the customer gets the bill, they will compare it to the quote. Yes, they were billed the amount promised, but none of the itemized amounts on the bill match the itemized amounts on the signed quote. Therefore, before the customer will pay, they need to know why their invoice does not match their quote; they need to make sure they got what they ordered and are not being ripped off with the pricing and part switches and so on.

The invoices become past due in the confusion and the company, in reality, has lost money on the job or the amount they made was not enough to warrant the effort of the sale.

How this company can correct this issue is by having the same people who install the job, quote the job. Only a true installation service person will know what they will or will not need to do the job. If they are going to install it, they should have a hand in the cost quote.

Another thing they can do is to break up large jobs like this into sections. Instead of giving one big, quote for the entire thing, one big job that takes weeks to do, break it up into smaller jobs. First, only quote the audio equipment in the boardroom, install and bill that. By breaking it up into smaller, manageable pieces, the company can then more accurately gauge the time and equipment needed.

The major problem with this company's billing procedure is the process where technicians hand in random scribbles on scrap paper as official billing documents. The business cannot expect a service technician, who is up to his/her elbows in grease or wiring and tools to stop and write down things on a piece of paper and be able to keep focus on their task. That is not practical. What results are inaccurate and illegible pieces of paper. Instead, there needs to be a service crew supervisor assigned to each job whose responsibility it is to ensure the installation report is followed and where it is changed, it is this supervisor's responsibility to accurately and neatly document that change accounting for all cost controls. That is not a job for a technician. With the responsibility placed on the supervisor, accuracy will improve.

This goes along with reducing empowerment in the company in any aspect that will affect the billing and receivables. Limited empowerment, to some degree, with clear accountability will improve the DSO.

CHAPTER FOUR – Value Based Collections

The first thing to remember is that the goal is to not have past due receivables to collect. Improving the credit policy will greatly improve the profit margin and and reduce the amount of past due receivables. However, in as much as there may be past due receivables to collect, this section will outline the value based collections method.

Value Based Management For Accounts Receivable

Key Points

The first key point to consider is consistency. Consistency is very important to collection efforts. There must be consistency with when billings are invoiced, when statements are mailed, when collection calls are made and when generally when each stage of the collection process is engaged. If there is no consistency, the customers will not react seriously to the billing and collection attempts and potentially, simply not respond.

The second key point to consider is following through. Any time a statement is made to the customer such as "If no payment is received by July 9th, then your account may be reported to the credit bureau as late in payments," then on July 9th, if no payment was received then that company's payments must be reported as stated. Even despite the word "may" being used, if word is given of any type of intent, that intent must be followed through upon. Whatever a company says they are going to do, that company must doe. Like the first key point, if this is not done, the customers will not react seriously to the billing and collection attempts and potentially, simply not respond.

Timeline

Building a collections policy timeline is a way to build structure in the credit and collections department so that both key points above are easier to manage. It will give a foundation to know what to expect and when. A structured timeline will ensure that the past due accounts are called in a timely manner, consistently and effectively. It will also ensure that each account receives appropriate follow-up and all pertinent people, internally and externally, are notified of the status of the accounts.

Here is a basic but sound timeline to reference:

Value Based Management For Accounts Receivable

✓ Invoices are sent out immediately either upon job completion or product delivery. Have a deadline for invoicing such as no later than 3 days after delivery or service completion.

✓ Five days after due date a reminder phone call is placed to the customer. Waiting 5 days is a good policy because most companies will actually mail the payment on the due date, so allow for mail time. During this phone call, remind the customer of the payment due and ask if the payment was mailed. If so, make note of how and when. If not, ask why and work to resolve the issues. Be friendly and build a relationship with the customer.

✓ 10 days after the due date, a late notice is mailed to the customer. This late notice will list the information consistent with the policies such as late fees assessed or interest due for non-payment. The late notice will demand payment in full immediately.

✓ 15 days past due date the second phone call is made to the customer during which information obtained during the first phone call is replayed to the customer in this call; such as reminding them of their payment promised or reminding them of the issues that have now been resolved, therefore payment should have been sent. Demand payment in full over the phone. During this phone call, be more firm and do not end the call without a promise to pay.

✓ The third phone call will be made on the day the customer promised to mail payment in full, call and find out if payment was indeed made.

✓ Twenty-five days after due date, a firm delinquent notice will be sent out. This letter will have a big red banner and the bolded words PAST DUE printed on it as well as the envelope. Make the account manager and/or sales person in charge of the account aware of the late balance and ask for their assistance in collecting the debt.

✓ 30 days past due, a phone call is placed to a senior level manager at the customer's place of business.

- ✓ At this point, make a phone call every three-business days to follow up on payments made.
- ✓ 40 days past due date a customized dunning letter is mailed outlining further actions that may be taken if no payment is received. Follow through on what is said may happen.
- ✓ Every three-business days continue making calls.
- ✓ Every 5 days send out a dunning letter.
- ✓ At 60 days past due consider what other steps need to be taken. This the stage where further action is required.

This is very basic timeline and should be used as a model to build upon a more extensive and customized collection timeline. Anything over 60 days past due is to be considered highly volatile, take the account outside of the normal timeline routine and begin to think outside the box. Each account will have to be evaluated individually to determine what will or will not be done. Is the account profitable despite the delinquency? If so, the company may not want to cut the account off. If not, then the company may want to cut it off. Is the equipment sold something the business wants to repossess? Is the business relationship one that encourages filing legal actions? At some point, the account will cease to be profitable due to the delinquency. At that point, that is where the account is shut off. Profitability is the key.

Basic Financial Principle

Pay attention to the time value of money. To illustrate, take the question *is receiving $2,000 today better than receiving $3,000 one year from now?* The answer is not necessarily. One would think so because receiving that $2,000 now is cash in hand now that can work towards building the company's equity and retained earnings and receiving that $2,000 now means the company has the cash now to invest. However, the time value of money lends to the demonstration that the receipt of $3,000 in one year may result in higher equitable returns.   To understand this, evaluate what the current value of $3,000 is today and the future value of $2,000 in one year. Use a simple TMV calculator and the current rates of investment interest.

For this example, the interest rate of 5% is used. That equates $2,000 in one year to be worth $2,100. It equates the current value of that $3,000 received in one year to be worth $2,800 today.

How this applies to credit and collections is that it demonstrates profitability in receivables lies in the value of the return not the age of the debt. All to often, credit and collections managers focus on the age of the debt when it may be more profitable to look at the time value of money in terms of receivables debt. What opportunity costs are being lost by not allowing that debt to carry on the books at an established and profitable interest rate? One key question here being, can the company afford to do this? Also, can the company afford not to do this?

Further Points

There is a collections industry adage, well known, "the squeaky wheel gets the grease," while that is true, keep in mind that if one wheel is squeaking then all the wheels are probably squeaking and none of them will stand out more than the others. What gets a company paid is not how often they bark, but how much value they are to the company owing them money. Therefore, it is imperative to become a high value to the customer. Later chapters will discuss more detail about how the company can do this, but remember hat if the customer has nothing to lose by not paying, they will not.

Utilize C.O.D. terms on problem customers or cut them off completely. Make sure these accounts are not being profitable in any way, do not cut off the money sources due to aging but realize that the company does not have to extend credit where they do not want.

On larger dollar invoices, consider taking an uncommon approach. Consider taking the amount due that is now showing up on the books and theirs as past due, and turning it into a promissory debt note on an installment payment plan with a personal guarantee of the business owner or CEO. For example, Jericho Inc owes Landover Corp $100,000 and it is approaching 90 days past due. Landover might offer Jericho a payment plan for that amount; maybe $33,333 payments per year with 8% interest, with a written promissory note that has a personal guarantee clause, signed by the owner/CEO. What this does is it takes that delinquent debt off Jericho's books as past due and turns it into current liabilities.

CHAPTER FIVE – Making Key Improvements

It's About Profit Not Aging

What is the number one mistake of credit and collections managers? It is a mistake that is so inundated in this genre of business that it is no longer perceived as a mistake, but instead is perceived as normal operating procedure. Repeatedly, this mistake is held up as the prime directive of the department, and it never should be. The number one mistake of credit and collections managers is the trend of focusing on the aging of the receivables as opposed to the profit level. What does this mean? The following is an example scenario.

Take for example, a credit and collections manager for a large supplier of office products. Now let us say this manager has a very large, national customer with multiple locations nationwide that he or she supplies all their office needs for and all of the bills are paid out of corporate under one account. Let us say for example that the customer orders $1,000,000 worth of product from this manager each year and average cost on those orders is around $250,000, so that customer is supplying the office supply company with $750,000 profit each year. Now let's say they are not the best at paying within terms of net 30, so the manager has given them net 60; but even that has not done the trick because they tend to have large receivable amounts beyond 4 months past due, let's even say that they have aging around 6 to 8 months past due. This is where most credit managers would put the account on credit hold until that balance is paid. This is incorrect.

The customer consistently orders $1,000,000 each year.

Value Based Management For Accounts Receivable

The profit on that $1,000,000 each year is $750,000.

This customer's aging looks like this:

Current	30+	60+	90+	120+	150+	180+
$25,000	$45,000	$67,000	$200,000	$150,000	$100,000	$413,000

On average, the office supply credit manager receives payments of $200,000 to $300,000 a month from this customer, most of which the customer earmarks for current debt, not past due.

Most credit managers would place this customer on hold until the 120, 150 and 180 balances are caught up but that is a mistake. This customer orders a lot from the office supply company and each month the office supply company receives a substantial payment. This is a long term, permanent customer and the office supply company is making tons of profit from them. The credit manager instead will want to take their monthly payments and continue selling to them, because although they are paying current debt and ignoring the late, they are paying and the profit margin is high, the office supply company can afford to let this customer go beyond terms because they are making a profit from them.

Any company is in business to make money that is the bottom line, which is the point.

Do not put accounts on hold if it will curtail the profit margin.

Pay attention to profitability over aging.

Another very important scenario that can be given is to imagine the credit manager of a tool dealership that sells mostly to factories. This credit manager has a new small to medium sized account that was new when the manager signed them, and this manager took a chance and gave them a line of credit. Now they are bankrupt and the tool dealership is out about $30,000 in unpaid receivables. The bankruptcy papers came through; their debt with the tool dealership is now void. The credit manager closes the account. Now this same company calls the credit manager back for a new order. Most credit managers would tell them no and send them packing. This is a mistake. What this credit manager will do is open up a new account for them on a cash only basis. If they can and are willing to pay cash for their tooling deliveries now that they have no debt, then do so.

Never turn down a paying sale, remember, it is about profit not aging.

Work accounts receivable files paying attention to profit not aging.

That tooling dealership credit manager would have in all likelihood made several collection attempts to that small to medium sized new client before the bankruptcy went into affect. The credit manager would have been focused on attention to detail for each call, however, perhaps failed to see the larger picture.

If the receivables team has to make collection calls to a certain company, then know that that receivables team is not the only receivables team calling that customer. If one bill collector is calling, then several other bill collectors are calling them also, perhaps as many as 30, 50 or 100 callers, depending on their size. The one single vendor out of many calling for payment? Because the 'squeaky wheel get the grease'? In a situation like this, there is not one wheel that will squeak more than the others. No vendor is standing out more than the others from the crowd.

Instead of trying to become the loudest wheel squeaking for payment, remember what this book explained earlier, that the primary objective is to increase the value to that customer. Collaborate with them and help them resolve their issues with their customers. The vendor who is paid over the others is the one who is a very big and key asset to their profits.

In order to begin understanding the approach to this, it is necessary to refocus on the basic accounts receivable needs. In order to be paid, it is necessary to have an understanding of the customer's internal structure and profit centers. It is necessary to know how they do things, understand their work routine and who the key players are. It is not meant to tour their company, although that would be an asset if possible. Learn the customer. Learning the customer cannot be accomplished by being an adversary. It is not done by calling with "This is Kim with such and such company; I'm calling to collect on invoice such and such that is past due."

That person the company is talking to, whether they are the owner, manager, clerk, buyer or project guru has other things to worry about and they do not need the caller adding to their stress. That is the number one reason traditional collections techniques fail.

Traditional collections techniques fail because they add to the stress of the company being called instead of alleviating them.

Even an accounts payable clerk, whose job it is to do nothing but enter invoices into the payment system all day, has a routine and task oriented job that requires them to focus on and a phone call regarding one invoice is simply an unwanted and uncooperative disruption.

Value Based Management For Accounts Receivable

Focus on becoming a joy and breathe of fresh air when making receivables calls. The outcome of this will alleviate their problems and help decrease their stress, not add to it.

No matter what the reason for their non-payment, the collector's approach is, that the reasons the customer has not paid is not the customer's fault. Therefore, ask the customer what is in their way to pay the invoice and how can assistance to them be rendered?

There will be a need for a certain entrepreneurial spirit in this approach. In the broader business sense, it has always been innovation and entrepreneurial thinking that has led profitability. Within the credit and collections genre, it is no different. Work to create the correct incentives in the relationship with client.

Focusing on profit and not aging will change which customers become priority, and therefore change the entire focus of service extended the clientele. This goes beyond the accounting department, remember that the accounts receivable books begin with the sales department. It is common in today's misguided business world to find that the structure of compensation towards the sales force actually is working against the profitability of the company. Sales clerks tend to focus on volume instead of quality and they tend to focus on the largest sized customers, not the ones who are most profitable.

Profitability does not necessarily go hand in hand with account size.

For example, a salesperson might have sold a new contract to the Worth Corporation with expected sales to be around $100,000 per year and that same salesperson might also have sold another contract to the Miner Corporation with expected sales to be around $25,000 per year; it can be expected that the salesperson will focus more on Worth then Miner. However, what if the profit made on the Worth sales was only 10% and the profit made on the Miner sales was 90%? If that turned out to be the case, then the sales clerk is losing money by not focusing on Miner as opposed to Worth.

Similarly, it might be that a company has a customer whose aging is $500,000 past due and another customer whose aging is only $10,000 past due, that does not mean that the company whose aging is $500,000 past due is less profitable than the other is; it is necessary to run the numbers to see which of the two is the real problem.

To repeat, it is about profit not aging.

On another level, focusing on profit and not aging will free employees from being mindless, policy following clerks and allow them to be independent thinkers who approach each client with a value-based initiative. If owners and managers can instill in employees the operative of looking for and creating value based profitable relationships with the clients, then those owners and managers will be spending less time making mundane and routine decisions as well as spending less time solving problems because the employees will have created an atmosphere that breeds prosperity.

High Versus Low Value

Keep in mind that credit does not have to be extended to every customer who applies regardless of credit rating. When credit is extended, the company extending that credit is giving away their product or service free until the customer decides pay, if they decide to pay. That is worth repeating, when credit is extended, the company extending that credit is giving away their product or service free until the customer decides pay, if they decide to pay

Value Based Management For Accounts Receivable

The more credit extended, the more profit has been given away. Whether or not the company charges interest is beside the point; the company can charge 30% interest if they want to or none at all, it makes no difference if they are never paid.

Business credit should be earned and it is perfectly acceptable to demand payment in full up front. Likewise, it is also perfectly acceptable to start each account with C.O.D. terms until a business relationship has been established and then move the customer to an open line of credit.

Larger more established companies will provide their prefabricated credit application and with expectations that their account will be opened with the highest limit available, simply because they are large and well known. Despite the size and desirability of this new potential client, what is important is how much daily operational value the products and services this new vendor contract will be to them. For example, no doubt a new sales contract to the Walt Disney World corporation would be very appealing. Landing a contract with Walt Disney World isn't easy, the Disney corporation has very strict guidelines that their vendors must adhere to in order to have the privilege of selling to them; and it is a privilege, don't misunderstand, having Disney as a customer is a very good thing. However, if someone were starting up a small business for the sole purpose of selling to the Disney theme parks, what should they choose to sell? Would they choose light bulbs or fishing tackle? Would they choose popcorn and funnel cake or toothpaste and denture cream? If the right value is presented to Disney in what is being sold to them then abiding by their credit requirements would be acceptable. However, if it is meant to sell them denture cream, and they actually place an order for this denture cream for some reason, it would be foolish to accept their credit terms, even though it is Disney, because even Disney prioritizes their bills and denture cream is not going to be high on their list of important debts.

Value Based Management For Accounts Receivable

Here are some examples of low value:

- Office Supplies To A Women's Shoe Store
- Printing Services To A Digital Information Company
- Auto Insurance To Residents Of New York
- Lawn Maintenance To A Hospital

Here are some examples of high value:

- Office Supplies To A Secretarial Services
- Printing Services To A Direct Mail Marketer
- Auto Insurance To A New York Taxi Company
- Lawn Maintenance To A Multi-Field Outdoor Sports Complex

The likelihood of any vendor being paid on time is greater from the examples of high value; those are the customers a company wants to focus on. The customers to whom low value is present, restrict those credit accounts or require C.O.D. from them regardless of who they are and how big.

Remember, credit is a privilege not a right, even for Disney. Moreover, that privilege comes from how they have honored the vendor's credit terms, not who they are. When operating under the Value Based Approach To Credit & Collections Management philosophy, there will be times when credit is denied to a particular potential customer and that company will call on the phone directly and demand to know why they have been denied. They will be shocked and honestly baffled. The reason for this goes back to the number one mistake of credit and collections departments and this new customer forgets that credit is a privilege and no vendor has to extend it, regardless. Having a profitable DSO begins with the credit policies. Do not take unnecessary risks with the extension of credit to customer accounts.

Value Based Management For Accounts Receivable

Nevertheless, do not make the mistake of assuming that once a value centered credit policy has been established, that the work is done. The continual monitoring of each account for credit limit adjustments is necessary and even mandated.

For example, a vendor might have extended a high credit limit to Center City Secretarial Service because they had a credit rating of nine and that vendor sells office supplies; but that does not guarantee that Center City will pay on time. What will happen to the profitability of the vendor's DSO with Center City Secretarial Service if Center City starts losing clients and therefore losing income? Center City will begin to pay slower and most likely, only partially. Assumptions of safety are never to me made. Put customers on credit hold if their profitability gets too far below the line of acceptability. Center City Secretarial Service might be that vendor's number one client, but they will soon become their number one problem if Center City goes default.

Monitoring credit involves keeping up with the news both nationally and locally. For example, that vendor might be aware that Center City has the contract for a large corporate office called Extreme LLC and then one morning the news reports that Extreme LLC is moving out of state. That vendor's time to take action is right then. They should adjust Center City's line of credit and call them to discuss how they are going to handle this large loss of revenue.

Value Based Management dictates that the customers of customers are just as important as the direct customer.

Credit worthiness lies beyond reputation and credit score; credit worthiness is something that is constantly and continually measured and measured and re-measured and adjusted, daily if need be. It's usefulness lies in value and just like the stock market, value changes daily.

Building Relationships With Customers

It is not enough to focus on value-based customers, make the right sales contracts and have the most optimal profit margins set upon them. In order for those value-based accounts to remain valuable, a good and strong relationship must be built with each and every one of them. A relationship that is unique to each one. An example of what is meant by unique to each and every one is when a salesman uses the same pitch on each account, that is not building a unique relationship and relationships built on that type of service will not have strong value. Building strong and unique relationships will work to increase sales and improve receivables.

So how are unique and value based relationships built? The answer is, it takes work, creative thinking and more work.

The first step is to maintain a regular level of communication with each customer. It is imperative that there are not long periods of time in between customer contacts. Keep in touch. If nothing more than just to say hi, this is very important.

Every vendor has those particular clients that place infrequent orders. That is okay. What is not okay is if those vendors are not maintaining a level of communications with these customers between sales.

The second step will sound so rudimentary that at first reading it will be dismissed as too simple. Do not do that. The dismissal of this rudimentary step is common place as it is expected to be obvious and automatic. It is obvious but it is not automatic at all. The second step is simply, be nice. Be the first to smile. Be the first to offer a hand. Be interested in their grandchildren or children. Find a reason to be impressed by them personally and express it. Do not be phony. Be genuine. The key to being nice is making them feel wanted, appreciated and admired.

The third step is acknowledgement without delay. When an email is received from the customer and the response to that email will require a day or two of information gathering, do not wait a day or two to respond to the email. Respond right away, acknowledge the receipt of the email and give an ETA on delivery of answer. When a phone message is received from a customer and the answer is not readily available, call that customer back anyway, discuss their question then let them know when they will call back with an answer. Acknowledge them without delay.

Other things that are suggested:

• Gift Giving - Chachkies
•Share Knowledge
•Go Above And Beyond Their Expectations
•Speak Their Language And Lingo
•Increase The Company's Involvement With Their Sales
•Be Reachable
•Be Approachable
•Be Friends Outside Of Business
•Anticipate Their Needs
•Follow Through
•Keep Promises
•Do Not Argue

Know Who The Customer Is

One of the most commonly made mistakes by even seasoned credit professionals is not knowing who their customer is. Understand this. It is key to know exactly who the customer is, what their legal name is, what type of business entity it is and who are the responsible parties in that business for the financial considerations.

For example, a vendor might set up a credit account for Rainbow Construction Inc in West End New Jersey, but send the bills to Rainbow Construction West LLC in New Lawn Virginia. That vendor might have it understood that the one in New Lawn is the parent company to the one in West End. Now the account goes severely delinquent owing hundreds of thousands; so the vendor engages in a lawsuit to try to recover their lost receivables. They sue Rainbow Construction Inc in West End New Jersey only to find out that is a DBA. Therefore, they sue Rainbow Construction West LLC in New Lawn only to find out that they are entirely owned by Rainbow Construction Corp Inc out of New York; and Rainbow Construction West LLC's lawyers instruct that vendor that the parent company in New York is not responsible for all their finances. Here is the catch, it is most likely that the vendor cannot sue Rainbow Construction Corp Inc out of New York because they never had any contract or signed credit terms with them.

A vendor has to know exactly who their customer is, who is responsible, what their legal name is and who has legal obligation to pay. Here is another, perhaps easier example to understand. Assume a vendor set up credit terms for East Omaha Ford Dealer in Omaha Nebraska and they default on the monies owed. Can they sue the Ford Company in Dearborn Michigan? No, they cannot because their contract was with this local franchise. Now, had that vendor gotten a signed agreement of parental credit with the HQ that would be different.

In most cases, however, parent companies are not so well known.

There once was a company that had a long-standing credit account with a vendor, this company was called WDL, Inc. The primary officers were Williams, Daniels and Lacey. When that account went belly-up the vendor tried to sue WDL, Inc only to find out there was no such firm, the real and legal name of the firm was Williams, Daniels and Lacey, Inc. That vendor failed to get correct legal name on the contract, therefore, when it came time for legal action, there was none available.

Who Is Doing The Dealing

Owner Or Career Manager

In terms of the owner or a career-minded employee/manager, they are essentially the same for these purposes; meaning someone who values their job as their career, especially if they are the manager or director, will require the same treatment as would be extended to the owner. They each take their jobs seriously and they each take it personally. That is very important to understand. What is said about their business or how they handle their department is what is said about them personally and they cannot be separated.

Do not begin by calling the owners and accusing them of not paying their bills. That would jeopardize the business relationship.

Value Based Management For Accounts Receivable

Owners are not going to delve into the basic routine of what their accounts payable clerks do for them. What this means is that the owner is not going to be able to check the status of a purchase order number. They do not have any clue what that purchase order number is, nor do they care. Their involvement is on a broader plane. They understand the projects going on that required materials and/or services from the company, but they have underlings to handle the details. Therefore, when a collections call is placed to the owner or manager, information is not requested, it is given.

To demonstrate the futility of placing a collection call to the owner or manager, the following is a typical dialog that would occur during such a call:

> Collector: "Payment for invoice 123 has not been received, can you pay that in full today?"

> Owner: "Invoice 123 has not been paid? Why not?"

When the owner asks "why not," that is a question they will actually expect answered to them instead of they providing the answer. Therefore, the technique used on the manager/owner is one quite opposite of the typical receivables call and because of this, will prove to be quite effective.

To understand why, know that what they are interested in is getting their projects completed so that they can make their money. Any hindrance in that will cost them money and that will become an immediate state of emergency requiring their full attention.

The optimal scenario is when that customer has been engaged in a long term project that requires payments based on stages of completion, or project payments. Let them know that the materials or services they very desperately require have not yet been shipped or began. They will ask why not, offering the opportunity to tell them the reason is because their employees (again state it so it is not their direct fault) have failed to provide payment on the past shipments or services rendered according to the terms agreed upon by the owner or manager themselves. Iterate to them that all the required information was given on the invoicing submitted more than once to their AP, even so, payment has not yet been received. At this point, the owner/manager should ask if communication has been extended to the AP department regarding this matter. Of course the answer will be yes followed by whatever information can be provided regarding that communication which did not lead to achieving a paid status.

In a less optimal situation, merchandise shipped or services provided to them were a onetime thing or at least not regularly scheduled and therefore do not have the advantage of holding future orders until paid. What then? Payment is achieved by providing the owner or career manager the motivation for paying the bill by appealing to their sense of control. Are they not aware that their employees have failed to do their task? During this call, provide the owner/ manager with evidence of all procedures to this point going off as they directed such as the order, delivery, purchase order manifests, signatures and such. Up to now however, they have been in control. Then stress that at this point, payment has not been received. Why not? Did they not intend to pay for this bill? Yes, of course they did. Then there must be something wrong in their accounting department and express relief at being able to bring this to their attention. This is a strong motivation. When an outsider brings to their attention an issue right underneath them that they were not aware of, that makes them angry and they will act upon it. It can be understood where they are coming from, they are the owner or manager and they are supposed to know what is going on, but they do not. That makes them look foolish. The owner and career manager has a lot at stake in their reputations and this is the driving factor that will get them to investigate the lack of payment.

Now play one more card. Call their underlings in the accounting department and mention that a conversation with the owner or manager just took place and that he or she seemed to have been taken by surprise by the current situation. Give the accounting department personnel a heads up that their boss is coming.

Bingo. It can be assured they will start doing what needs to be done before the boss comes down the hall.

Just A Job Clerk

Not every call will be placed to the owner or manager. Some if not most calls will be placed to the accounts payable clerk and that clerk 'just works there.' It is just a job to them. They come in everyday, punch a time clock, count the minutes to the next 15-minute break until it is time to go home and they do their job dreaming of Maui. This person will not respond to the same approach described above. They are not the ones making the millions when the company gets the project done, they make the same hourly wage if it succeeds or fails; it is the boss who gets rich, they just work there.

When talking to this clerk, the key is to make them feel appreciated. Make them feel that they are the only ones in that entire place with any common sense or know- how. Why can the company not put them in charge? Things sure would be done faster. This person will state that the invoice has not been processes because not all the things are in place that will allow them to process it. Understand that; the invoice has not been paid because things are not in place that allows them to pay it. This will be the answer every time, they have procedures to follow that require certain things to be in place before they can post payment and if the invoice is not paid it is only because those certain things have not been achieved. At this point, paying the invoice is beyond their limitations. If a relationship is not established with them, that is where it will end.

However, regardless of what the clerk says, they do have the power to move things along in order to get the invoice paid. So how is a relationship established with them? By appealing to their need to be appreciated and understood. This person is going to come in everyday complaining about the same things repeatedly, of where they work. This person never files things right, that person never gets the right authorizations, this person never completes their paperwork, that person is never in their office.

During the conversation with them, these sentiments will be expressed in their statements, one way or another. Sympathize. Express mutual conditions and strike a chord with them.

The next step is to give them what they need to pay that invoice. That which is needed by that clerk to solve the problems at hand and get the invoice paid is empowerment. Give the clerk empowerment. Give this clerk empowerment by allowing him or her to understand what resolution is needed and how it is to be obtained and then making them feel empowered to do so.

To relate, there is a story of a man and his time in Vietnam during that war. Seems his platoon was walking through the jungles on the way to secure a location for some helicopters when they were suddenly ambushed by hostile fire. At this time, they were not that far from their location. They radioed in their location and the situation at hand to command. They were given orders to backtrack and take a route that would enable them to meet up with another platoon, change course and head to the location they needed to secure via another route, and still make it in time to their destination. Doubled with this other platoon they were expected to be able to handle the enemy fire. This command was given by the authorities who were safe back at headquarters who had never actually stepped foot into this area. Although they had very detailed maps and a clear understanding of the grounds, still, they had never been there. His platoon attempted to follow these orders, even radioing the other platoon and arranging a rendezvous point, all the while shooting and being shot at. What was not understood by command was that little low lying area that ran right through the jungle they were in was connected to a drainage canal that was fed by farm fields. There had been tons of rain in the days past. This created a swamp deep enough to drown a man, filled with poisonous life forms. His platoon stood a better chance facing the enemy fire. However, quickly, the platoon saw a way around the situation, which required them to veer off towards an entirely different direction, and they still would have been able to make their location by the required time, however doing so, they would not be rendezvousing with the other platoon nor would they be following orders of command. The Lieutenant of his platoon radioed in their change in course and was told not to change course. Just then, the Lieutenant was shot and so his direct report. The platoon needed to act quickly. Either they take this other route, which was the best thing to do or head into the swamp, which was what they were told to do. The enemy knew that water was there and knew that if they headed into it, at least half would not make it out, making it easier for the enemy to pick the rest of them off. This is what they wanted. The platoon had a problem but they did not have the empowerment to do what they needed to do to fix the problem. They had the solution, they knew what to do and they just did not have authority to do so. At this point, a few men in the platoon turned to a fellow soldier who had no more rank than they had, but had more field and battle experience, and told him it was his responsibility to make the decision and lead the platoon out. Of course, this soldier questioned why they thought he had the authority to do so and they explained to him that unless he chooses to do something and take charge, they would all surely die. That was all the motivation he needed, he stood up and took command, empowering himself to change course. They took the alternate route and got out of their alive. They veered off course and made it alive, the remaining ones, to their destination.

The clerk to whom the call is placed, is no different from that soldier who stood up and took charge. That soldier was not in charge and had no authority, but he knew what needed to be done and the best way to do it. That clerk is the same way. Merely by discussing the matter with that clerk and allowing him or her to come to the understanding that they and only they fully understand what is going on, and therefore because they and only they fully understand the situation, it is they and only they who can fix it. That is giving empowerment to that clerk to do what is needed, to enable payment of the invoice as opposed to simply replying, "Sorry I can't pay this, I don't have such and such yet from so in so." Make them take responsibility for the resolution, make them commit to it and follow up with them.

Empowering the clerk in this manner makes the issue personal to them. This changes things completely, it changes it from "this is what is going on in this company and I get paid either way so I don't care" to "I understand what is going on, I have the power and knowledge to fix it and I am being held accountable to do so." In that way, things will begin to get moving.

People are more than just their job; they are people with real issues, real dilemmas and real lives. Making a call to a company to collect a bill will result in nothing. Making a call to 'Bill' or 'Jill' at the customer's business to assist in problem resolution will yield better results.

Connecting With The Customer

Connect with the customer. Even the most delinquent and hard customers can be connected with on a gainfully, mutually beneficial benevolent relationship.

To be successful at connecting, it is required that connection be achieved with the customer each communication, each time.

When talking to that accounts payable person, put them in the position of feeling as if they owe a favor. This is achieved by giving them something useful and beneficial and extending this gift to them first. Perhaps the reason the invoice is not being paid is that there is a problem with the purchase order number and/or the buyer who issued it. The accounts payable clerk is having trouble gaining cooperation. Initiate a 3-way call and hand that buyer to the payables clerk. By doing so, a gift has just been given to them and compelled them to feel the need to reciprocate.

Perhaps the reason the payables clerk isn't paying the invoice is because they cannot get clearance for the balance in full, negotiate with them and offer to clear part of the balance away, allowing them to take credit for reducing their companies outflow. Whatever the situation is, first make the connection by giving them some sort of 'gift' that will cause them to feel they are now owing a favor back.

Another valuable technique in connecting with the customer is to verify and validate the policies and notions that the customer already has in place. An easy example of this is service charges. Some companies do not pay service charges. If it is told to that company that service charges will be extended and it is expected that they break their policy and pay them, this will result in a severely delinquent account, most likely all in service charges.

Instead, validate to that company their policy of not paying service charges and communicate to them a wholehearted acceptance of this; this is establishing a connection with that customer.

Connecting with the customer over accounts receivable issues will also depend on the necessity to portray a position of authority and knowledge. People are not likely to connect with someone they feel is wasting their time. By contrast, people are likely to connect to someone they view as having authority and knowledge. The affect of doing so comes with a tone of voice and vocabulary that exudes professionalism, empowerment and accountability. Most would be more cooperative talking to the credit and collections manager of a company than the department filing clerk and would expect that manager to sound like a manager, not a filing clerk.

Finally, the most effective way to connect to the customer is to match to them in personality and style. If they are laid back and casual, then that is the persona to adopt; likewise, if they are in a hurry and only wants to hear the bottom line, then that is what is done. Whether the conversation is being conducted with a career minded person, a college student who is only there part time, someone from the east coast or someone from Arizona, it doesn't matter who they are, become them.

Customer Accounts Payable Assistant

One of the key features of the Value Based Approach To Credit & Collections Management is to understand that what once was the norm, no longer is. From here, everything changes.

Value Based Management For Accounts Receivable

The first thing to do is change hats. Remove and throw away the 'accounts receivable hat.' Put on the hat of a 'customer accounts payable assistant.' What is the difference? As an accounts receivable person, the focus is on bringing in the coinage for the company, oblivious to the needs of the customer. By contrast, as a customer accounts payable assistant, the main purpose is to make the customer's life easier, and solve their problems so that they are free to process the invoices appearing on their desk.

The Roman diplomat Cicero said, "A problem well stated is a problem half solved" and nothing could be truer in credit and collections. What is required is gaining the pertinent information from the customer in order to state well what that which is the problem.

If it were as easy as calling and reminding the customer to pay, there really would be no need for collection agencies or late notices. What is necessary is in order to get them to pay is problem solving, each and every time.

Reward Them For Keeping In Touch

Every now and then, the customer will actually call their creditors voluntarily when they are behind in their debts. The purpose of their call is to state why they are not going to be able to pay their bill. This does happen. Sometimes a company honestly cannot pay, even though they had every good intention.

Do not discourage a company from keeping in touch; encourage this behavior. This means that when the customer calls to explain why they cannot make payment, do not hard collect on them. Soften up, lighten up and be cheery and understanding. If this is their first time calling, certainly give them the time they need to pay and be agreeable about it.

It will be required to determine how many times a customer will be able to call and state they cannot pay before they are told no. However, the key idea here is to do everything possible to encourage them to keep in touch.

It is very rare that if a true deadbeat who does not intend to pay at all, regardless of whether or not they can, will call just to state such. Most of the time, the ones calling are the ones who truly do want to pay, so it is best to find a way to work with them. In the future when their cash flow is more positive, this will reflect on an increase in sales.

One way to work with them is to set up partial payments. Any payment amount received is a good thing. Moreover, the payments do not have to be large; they only have to be something. Most of the time, it makes the customer feel better that they are paying any amount, even a small one, until they can swing the cash flow to pay the balance. Receiving payments is what is desired and it extends excellent customer service that brings in more customers.

Hardball is not always the best tactic, in fact, it rarely is.

Value Based Management For Accounts Receivable

Training The Customer To Pay

New customers need training, just like new employees. It is a partnership, an understanding, and both sides must come to terms with what is expected. The first thing that must be done is to apply any special billing requirements the customer may have to their invoices and statements. Before the customer can be trained, their needs and requirements must first be met and in full and with 100% accuracy.

Regardless of whether the invoice is net 30 or 60 or net 10/30, one key way to train the customer is to call them ten days before the bill is due and ask them if everything is in line for the processing of the invoice. This offers the opportunity to resolve any issues that are present before they cause the bill to be delinquent. It also allows the opportunity to learn the customer.

Another thing to do is obtain key personnel and/or department head email address and send them friendly 'heads up reminders' when the bill is about to be due. Send it 'receipt requested,' even if they do not send a reply receipt, it is understood that when that email popped up in front of them, it required them to click 'yes' or 'no' and thereby drew their attention to the matter. It forces them to notice the email, even in this small way.

On Customers that are typically late, do not wait for the delinquency to occur before calling them. Give them a pre-delinquent courtesy call.

Understand that most of the time the invoicee does not read the net terms the same as the invoicer. When the invoicer bills net 30, to them that means that they receive the money by the 30th day after the date of invoicing. However, that to them means the invoicee is that the payment process begins at 30 days, causing the invoicee to not be paid until net 45, at the earliest. Other times, customers ignore the net terms completely and say that when they are paid by their customer they will pay their vendor.

Never let this be allowed. As stated before, it is very irrelevant when they are paid. They agreed to the terms of sale when taking out an account and placing the order and those terms did not allow for the unseemliness of how they handle their own receivables. They have a debt, and that is that.

When calling an account for payment, and being told "the check is in the mail," mark the account to call them exactly ten days after the date the "check was put into the mail."

Now here is the kicker, in 11 days if payment has not been received, call them back. Not in 12 days, but 11. Talk to the same person as before and remind them that 11 days ago and all was fine, however here it is 11 days later and still no payment. Insist on payment over the phone.

Offering the customer incentives for paying on time is also another method to employ. Businesses of all sizes, even consumers, love to take advantage of discounts and will go out of their way to do so. For example, if the terms are net 30, offer the customer a discount for paying with net 20.

In order to train the customer, what is needed is to instill in them accountability. In order to do this, acquire an accounts payable contact that has the empowerment to make decisions. Form a relationship with that accounts payable person so that when the time comes to push, pushing is done directly on them, and yes, make it personal. That is paramount to training the customer.

One key and very important element in training the customer is doing following through on statements given to the customer, whether they were verbal or written. Do not ever make empty threats or fail to follow through on what was said might be done. Do not use the words 'may' or 'might.' It is common for past due notices to have a statement similar to "If the amount is not paid further action may take place." This is a mistake. If an invoice, statement or letter being sent to the customer says something to the effect of "if payment is not received then there may be legal action taken" then the credibility of the company has just been lost because the customer knows the statement is most likely a bluff. The rule is that whatever is stated or even implied must actually be carried out. If an invoice, statement or letter being sent to the customer says something to the effect of "if payment is not received then there may be legal action taken" then if payment is not received, initiate legal action, no hesitation, no maybes. In reality, this is most likely not really the desired action and that is why it is imperative that warning statements are never given unless it is the true fact that they will be carried out. The customer must come to realize that there are no false warnings.

Make Them Want To Pay

The customer has been contacted, their problems have been solved that relate to the billing. The receivables clerk that called them, AKA the customer accounts payable assistant, has also managed to de-stress their day. Perhaps they have eliminated hours of accounting reconciliation for the customer, and therefore have removed the roadblocks that stand in the customer's way in paying the invoice. So now, they should pay, right? That is right for half the customers. The other half still will not pay, simply because they do not want to. Really, sometimes it simply comes down to that, they just do not want to. It does not matter the reason behind this sentiment, it is not as licentious as it may seem. It is simply a matter of priorities and time.

Value Based Management For Accounts Receivable

So now, the next step is to get them to want to pay. Make them see the bill as a priority to take time for. To do this, put inside them a desire to want to pay that invoice.

There are a few things that can be done to achieve this. As previously mentioned, one of the things that can be done to make them want to pay, and it is done very commonly, is offer a discount for prompt payment. If terms are net 30, print on the invoices 10% discount for paying within net 20. Many of the customers will take advantage of this and will automatically deduct 10% off the total bill when they send a remit. This is a very popular method and it does spark the initiative to put these invoices ahead of the others who do not offer discounts. The primary objective to offering prompt payment discounts is that it cuts into the profit margin, which may be a very small margin to begin with. This fact cannot be argued with, it does cut into the profit margin. However, it also gets the bill paid and it need not be pointed out that an unpaid bill cuts even deeper.

Another common method used is bonus incentives. Offering the collection team bonus commissions on the amounts they collect will also work to get the customer to want to pay. The reason is very fundamental; it is the receivables team that actually builds the relationship with the customer and it is the receivables team that gets to know them. Instinctively they will learn how to interact with the customer on the most optimal level and the bonus commission they earn will encourage them to make that call with the true goal of gaining payment as apposed to simply making the call as part of their job routine. If the collector gets paid the same whether or not the customer pays their bills, where is the incentive to push the customer to pay? Set collection goals based on where it is desired to have them be and offer a bonus whenever that goal is met.

Value Based Management For Accounts Receivable

One simple and very powerful thing to do is send thank you gifts. When a customer does pay the invoice promptly, send them a hand written thank you note and if at all possible include a small, inexpensive token gift, perhaps something along the lines of mints or free pens with the company name on them or sticky notes. This might seem quirky, but do not be surprised at the effect it has on the payables clerk who will become accustomed to getting and using the gifts.

Any incentive scheme can work as long as it is a combination of reward, recognition and immediate, positive feedback both on a personal and corporate level. Offering a 10% discount, for example, is a good incentive, but it does not work on everyone because it lacks one element: making that accounts payable clerk who writes the check feel recognized and appreciated. It is a sad fact that many Americans go to work hating their jobs. There is no appreciation extended to them for doing their jobs. Offer that to them.

Successful accounts receivable is about more than billing and invoicing and posting payments. It is about relationship building in a method that equates to a positive appreciation towards the customer. That boils down to correctly invoicing them, yes, but also resolving their issues, offering incentives and making them feel appreciated.

Value Based Management For Accounts Receivable

Know Why They Are Not Paying – Is It Short Cash Or Not A Priority

Cash flows through a business on a continuing basis although there are times and circumstances when the outflow exceeds the inflow. In a new venture, the expense of asset purchases will not be immediately returned by way of cash income. Instead, the funding for a new business will likely take the form of owner investment or long-term borrowing from a bank and the principal will be paid back by future profits. Both of these scenarios are challenges that will affect the receivables when collecting from a new business. The other challenge that may be seen in a new venture account is the depletion of capital due to a period of operating losses and all new ventures will have operating losses in the interim. This type of situation is unlikely to be remedied by any borrowing of funds since banks will not fund a loan to cover losses. The cash will have to come from outside investment or from the sale of any unneeded assets, or the lobbying against debt owed, which is the most likely. Meaning, they will avoid paying the bill. One of the things to look at in determining if in the long haul, this new venture will be worth the risk is to find out how they handle the retaining of profits. When a new company has a prolonged period of profits that creates a positive cash flow, it is usually the first inclination and the one most often taken by those who fail in their business venture to increase the salaries or draws for themselves and perhaps other managers or put the money directly into growing the business. Those are mistakes. One of the things an intelligent new venture owner will do is take the profits and put them into an accessible money market account. A business out of cash is a business out of choices. Watch for overspending and no investing.

Value Based Management For Accounts Receivable

Play It By Their Rules

One of the key mandatory rules to establish as part of the credit policy is: that every account that is set up is set up with all the customer's requirements in place.

What that means is if the customer requires a purchase order number on an invoice to be paid, then set up the account so that no order can be taken without a purchase order number and no invoice can be created without a purchase order number. However, not just any purchase order number, the correct purchase order number. A great percentage of unpaid bills are due to lack of the correct purchase order number in place, and an even greater percentage of no purchase order number at all.

It is inevitable that if an error can be made it will be made. Create an atmosphere that makes it hard for those errors to be made.

Purchase orders are not the only requirement the customer might need. There are others, such as restrictions on who can place orders. If the customer says that only certain employees can place orders, then set up the account so that only certain customer employees can place orders. Do whatever the customer needs done in order to eliminate issues in the future that will prevent the bill from being paid.

It makes no difference the size of the customer, large or small, if the customer's billing requirements are not met, then the bill will not be paid. A purchase order number ensures for the customer that the right person who has the authority to place orders has done so, with permission and allocated funds already set aside. As a supplier, encourage purchase order numbers from all the customers.

Value Based Management For Accounts Receivable

At first, it might seem like a hassle, especially for smaller, less structured companies, to ensure all these parameters are in place, especially across each different client file. Nevertheless, do not hesitate and do not be afraid to put the effort into policing the employees to make sure these needs are met.

Dealing With Very Large Companies

Sometimes when dealing with very large companies, none of the approaches described above will work. Often times, this large company will have their suppliers entering invoices for payment into an online invoicing system. In this method, the data is entered and uploaded online, it enables the vendor to check the status of payment online, and even allows the vendor to input help desk tickets for problem resolution online towards the issues of past due invoices and all this can be done without ever speaking to a human.

If things go well, then the online system can save time, money and energy. However, it is quite possible that payment is being delayed by this large company and the online system just is not giving the answers needed. In reality, that accounts payable department is probably hundreds big and in several different locations with no communication between them. How can a supplier deal with an accounts payable department like that? Simply, do not.

Do not call the accounts payable department at all. In a situation like this, revert to the purchasing department, the exact person whom issued the purchase order number and/or placed the order.

In a large company like this, a buyer is assigned to a project. The project manager gives the buyer a list of materials needed for the job and the buyer prices the materials and negotiates pricing, delivery and service quotes. They then give these quotes to the management who approves the sum total and issues a purchase order number for these materials for this project. That buyer then contacts the supplier and places the order, they offer the purchase order for the invoicing and additionally all the other billing requirements.

Even when the supplier complies without error to all this, it can be found that the bill is 60 days out and unpaid.

Hold that buyer accountable for the fact that the bill is still not paid and do so in such a way that hinders all their other purchasing privileges, making them resolve the issue quickly.

That buyer who issued the PO#, if called for payment of the delinquent invoice, they will give the run around and advise to call accounts payable, he or she is on the buying side and they do not issue checks, they will say. That is true. However, that is not the answer to accept. The key here is to understand the daily work routine of that buyer. That buyer is sitting in an office loaded down with paperwork and reports and a ringing phone and emails coming in by the score. They are getting emails and calls from vendors. However, the real calls that they focus on are the calls from the project managers. Those are the calls that drive them up the wall. Project managers have a deadline, they have many deadlines and they live and breathe by. They cannot and will not fall behind because that increases the cost of the project and that would be a poor performance on their part. They need these materials when they need them without any issues.

What would happen if that project manager were told that no more deliveries would be given to them because their buyer is failing to do his or her job right? What has just been done is to create one angry and stressed project manager. Whom is that project manager going to call about this? That is right, the buyer.

Value Based Management For Accounts Receivable

Basically this technique utilizes the common concept of credit hold, however in a non-traditional way. This is getting right to the heart of the matter, the project manager, and creating a tornado around them. That tornado is going to swirl from the project manager to the buyer who will then in turn contact the accounts payable department themselves to find out what the holdup is.

Whatever it is, the buyer will see it through to resolution and get the bill paid.

Know whom to call when.

Sometimes the call isn't placed to accounts payable to collect on a bill. Place the call to whoever would feel the urgency the direst. Usually, that is the project manager.

Checking Out The Customers Of Customers And Why This Is Necessary

Regardless the genre of business, it can be assured that the customers of the customers are more important to them then their vendors. What this means is that if their customers are dissatisfied and are not paying, then the business' receivables will be delayed. There is a circle of life in the business world that works its magic every day.

Therefore, despite the fact that it is not allowed to accept the excuse for non-payment of "when I am paid, you will be paid" from the customer, even so, pay attention to the customers of your customer. By doing this, it will gain an added advantage over the competition. This will sound like an uncommon idea, and it is. All business-to-business accounts receivable clerks will eventually hear the excuse, "when I am paid you will be paid." Commonly, the typical response to this is to explain that terms are net 30 and the sale was not a three way deal; their relationship with their customers is their issue and has nothing to do with the late invoice for which the call is about. Sometimes this will work, it should always be the first response, but it will not work all the time.

Therefore the new approach is to say the opposite and care that their customers have not paid them and offer assistance help the customer improve their situation. Why? To be paid. That is the point, is it not? If the financial health of the customer were good, then by reasoning their business with their vendors would be good and similarly if their financial health is poor then their relationship with their vendors will be poor as well. This novel approach adds value to the relationship with the customer and it greatly benefits them. By helping the customer improve their bottom line, this adds an additional service to the business relationship that competitors cannot provide. This is invaluable.

In order to do this, it requires a unique frame of mind. Under normal circumstances, the line is drawn between the customer and the customer's customer; that is quite understandable. Should a vendor wait for the customer to be paid, the vendor may never be paid. After all, the vendor has no idea of the type of credit policy the customer has nor can the vendor control it. Now, however, it is important to have say so in order to aide them in keeping clean with their past due. From now on, envision the customer as part of the team, part of the company and their customer is who the team is going after. Treat the company's customer not like a customer but like a business partner and this will greatly improve the entire bottom line, for the team.

Absolutely be aware that this is a slow process to grow. It will take time in order to fully implement this idea, allow the change to be slow because the effort is not only trying to change the way the company does things but also the way the customer does things as well. Do not alienate them, instead slowly gain their trust to this idea.

With that, how does the company implement this idea?

Begin by prioritizing the company's customer database. Begin with the one that earns the most dollars and work down the list, one by one, revamping how business is conducted with each customer. Make a customized, tailored approach that serves their needs to their customers.

For example, recall the previous examples of the Nitrous Oxide distributer and the dental office. Under normal circumstances, it would be that deliveries would be made on a weekly basis for a set amount of filled Nitrous Oxide tanks to the dental office and in doing so, also pick up empty cylinders. Deliveries would be around back and the tanks would be brought into the back office room leaving the dental assistants to manage the rest. Under this new approach, carry this service farther and extend service to the company's customer's customer. Instead of just dropping off full cylinders and picking up empty ones, carry each full cylinder to each dental chair, install it, regulate it, manage its mechanical needs and sterilize the equipment that extends from the tank to the patient. It can also be added to this service to manage the billings of Nitrous Oxide for the dental office and by doing so, administrative profitability has been increased for the customer by freeing up this task for the. The value here lies in the integration of the company into the customer's business, giving a stronger foothold into customer loyalty and value. However, more importantly, by managing the Nitrous Oxide billings for the dental customer, the company is effectively managing their receivables and the customers of the customer.

However, the real value would be in that hobby store customer who only pays once per year for their annual rocket sales event and pays three to six months beyond terms. How can the business extend itself to their customer's customer in this situation, so that the value is recognized to both? Do this by making the customer a partner in the services instead of just a customer. The hobby store customer will have clientele that will find the Nitrous Oxide useful for their rocketing. Where do they get their Nitrous Oxide? Not from the hobby store. However, why not? Collaborate with the hobby store and allow them to become a sales site dealer for the different gases, compounds and chemicals their customers would find useful. The company handle the delivery and set up for the customer and they get part of the sale proceeds. Now the company has increased their value to the hobby store customer and have increased their revenue, and by extension the receivables.

Integrating the customer into a partnership role that services their customers jointluy will improve profits as well as the business relationship . The value here is that the company's reach has just been greatly increased in which its business can serve potential clients by sharing resources. The joint effort is felt by the customer in the business cycle of life and the company's link in the chain has just extended, increasing profits. Indeed, there is no limit to just how far down the chain this approach can go.

This method not only improves receivables but it has the added side effect of being able to improve profits without cutting costs. This has a positive motivational effect on employees, partners and customers. Better quality, better service and better profits.

The key to controlling profitability is to enable the customer to better manage their customers.

Each customer this plan is implemented on will have its own unique needs and therefore the basis of the partnership will differ. This requires rebuilding the partnership model with each new customer. Begin by looking beyond the customer and identify factors where the product or service extends to their customer. In what ways could the customer's customer receive better benefits, value and service that would bring profitability to the company and customer? Find that need and service it.

By paying attention to the customer's customers, it will be that the company's sales department will take on an entire new role of business development, not in hitting the pavement and finding new clients but in extending their current client's reach. Sometimes, the most profitable company is not the one with the most customers, but the ones with the most important ones. This plan can build that for the company.

This new strategy of making the customers business partners instead of customers will also work to increase the customer's satisfaction with the company and this is very valuable to being paid and being paid on time. An example can be explained in the common customer survey/comment card. Send them out to all of the customers and ask them to rate the company on a scale of good to bad in several different areas. When the cards are returned, tally up the vote and look at the percentages. It might be found that 89% of the customers find the company perfectly satisfactory. However, what about that 11% that did not? How do they affect the profitability? That 11% affects the profitability in a stronger, more detrimental way than the 89% that favored the company because it is that 11% that is brings the profitability down. By promoting those 11% of customers from simply customers to business partners, that will turn that 89% into 100%. The profit margin will be beautiful.

Newly Delinquent Accounts

If sales terms are net 30, then an account is past due at 31 days. If sales terms are net 60 then an account is past due at 61 days. If sales terms are net 10 prox., then an account is past due on the 11th day of the following month.

Even the best customers must honor the company's sales terms. Even when there has been a business relationship with the customer for years, the customer still must be expected to keep to the terms. If they are billed on net 30 then they need to pay on net 30.

This is a very good moment to bring up another point. Just as it is not to be done to extend the same credit limit setting terms to each customer, it is also not recommended to extend the same billing terms to each customer. For those customers that have been faithful customers for years, then reward them. If standard terms are net 30, and then give this special customer net 60 terms. Doing this will let them know they are appreciated. They will be less likely to use another vendor and it eliminates awkward collection call moments to a customer who is greatly valued.

However, newly delinquent accounts are handled, how they are handled is paramount to the installation of preventing future write offs. Issues in billing are like a fire, the longer the waiting period to put out the fire, the hotter and more wild that blaze grows and the closer to impossible it will be to control it, or at the least, when it is controlled, damage will have already been done. When an invoice or account first goes past due, approach it with a problem solving mentality. It is not desirable to call and play hard collections, instead assume there is a viable and curable reason the customer has not yet paid. Call to assist them in handling this issue. People by nature will be more responsive to those who identify with their needs and this holds true in the business world when it should be a simple matter of black and white numbers. The numbers are the discussion points in what is to be done however; the tools of the trade are gentle persuasive techniques to get the accounts payable person to open up and cooperate on resolution.

Some Of The Situations That Will Be Encountered

Situation One: They Don't Send A Remit With Payment

A payment comes from the customer and it was simply a check and no remit. The balance on their account is $1500 made up of 10 invoices of different amounts and the check received was $500. It can be assumed it is for the oldest invoices, or it can be assumed it is for any invoices that add up to $500 evenly or it can be assumed it is simply towards the general balance. If any of these notions are assumed, that is not only incorrect but it creates future accounting issues. The customers must be trained to send a remit with each payment. When payments are received without a remit then pick up the phone and call them and discuss with them what they want that specific check applied to. Then apply it as they instruct and no other way. Follow up with an updated statement.

Situation Two: The Credit Was Already Used

This scenario usually is created by not having handled scenario one correctly, in the past. The customer sends a check along with a remit advice that utilizes a credit invoice along with their check, however, for whatever reason it is discovered that the credit has already been applied and is not available. Most company's right will apply what they can of the check and short pay the last invoice listed on the remit advice and leave it at that. That is a mistake, and it is not advisable. Nor is it extending any kind of decent customer service to the customer. Before applying any of the check, pick up the phone and call that payables department and discuss with them the reason the credit was not available and get new instructions on how to apply that check. Apply it as they instruct and no other way. Follow up with an updated statement.

Situation Three: They Send A Remit But The Amount Is Short

Any time the customer short pays an invoice, barring simple accounting errors on their end, there is a specific and very good reason. The reasons could be anything from their being over charged, or they could have a policy in place they do not pay fuel charges and the company invoice lists a fuel charge. It is not possible to list what all the reasons will be that a customer will short pay an invoice, but they will, and the times they do will be many. Again, pick up the phone and call that payables department and discuss with them the reason for the short payment, resolve the reason for the short payment and get new instructions on how to apply that check. Apply it as they instruct and no other way and then send them an updated statement.

Situation Four: They Over Pay

There will be times, although not as many as the short payments, that the customer will over pay. Most companies will pay the listed invoices and then put the remaining amount on the account as a credit or they will go ahead and pay other invoices. Both of these things are a big mistake. Paying other invoices is a larger mistake than simply applying a credit. A company will not simply send random amounts of cash for no reason, if they overpay then that is a clue that their books and the company's books are not in sync. However, like the situations above, pick up the phone and call that payables department and discuss with them the reason for the over payment and resolve the issues that caused the over payment and get new instructions on how to apply that check. Apply it as they instruct and no other way and then send them an updated statement.

Payments must be applied exactly as the customer instructed, and only as they instructed. Any time that their remit advise cannot be followed to the cent, it is an indication that their books to not match the company's and that is the issue needing attention. Once these issues are fixed, then as long as the payments are always applied as the customer instructs, there should be no further issues in this regard.

Red Flags

Red flags are indicators to an experienced professional that tells them there is something wrong and the customer is short of cash. These are some examples of red flags:

- Accounts payable voice mail box is full
- They don't respond to contact attempts
- A lot of change-over in their accounts payable departments
- Returned mail
- Broken Promises
- They never seem to receive the invoices or statements
- Their computers are always down or being updated

By contrast, a customer may have the money to pay but they still are not dong so. This is an example of the invoice not being a high priority on their schedule. Once it has been established that the company's bills are being ignored due to not being a priority, it is time to pull in the reins on that account and shift it to COD. Utilize stronger arm tactics such as repossession or legal collections. In situations such as this, the only way the invoice will be paid is by increasing the priority of the bills. If the invoices/products are not a high value to their company then the only way to will manage this is to make the lack of payment on the debt threatening.

Post Payments Correctly If No Remit Call Them

One of the most common responses that will be heard, especially from long-term customers, is that the invoice in question was already paid with check number such-and-such. When looking up check number such-and-such, it is found that indeed that check was received but it paid other invoices.

This is caused by a history of not applying the customer's payments as was instructed. Hopefully the issue will not be a longly historical one, because a call to the customer must be placed in order to straighten out the confusion.

These scenarios are always the same, the receivables team feels that the customer's payables team has no clue what they are doing and the customer's payables team feels that the vendor's receivables team has no idea what they are doing. The payables team is right and the receivables team is wrong, regardless of the black-and-white facts. Even in cases where the payables team sent payment for invoice such and such and then a month later sent another payment for that same invoice, receivables is still wrong if they apply that payment elsewhere.

Send Delinquent Notices To Account Managers As Well As Sales Team Members Within The Company

Not every collection effort extended will be to the customer. It is recommended to also make collection calls for past due accounts to the sales teams and/or account managers within the company. The ideal situation would be that the sales teams are not paid until the account they sold pays their bills. In other words, they should not earn commission based on the sale, but on the payment of the sale.

However, this unfortunately is not always going to be the case, even though it is the best policy. Therefore, it becomes necessary to alert the sales team and account managers when an account is past due and involve them in getting the account paid.

The first few times the salespersons are alerted that an account is past due, predictably, what their response will be is " . . . so, collect it, isn't that your job?" The answer to this is 'yes', and that is exactly what is being done. Then go on to explain that this is an account they worked hard to build a relationship with and that this is an account that if it is nurtured right could earn that sales person future high commissions. What is detrimental to their future income with this client is the fact that receivables now has to get involved to collect their bill. Make them understand that it is in their best interest to become involved and get this bill paid so that their future income is not hindered with bad debt collections and write-offs. In other words, hit them where their heart is, their wallets.

Once an understanding has been established with the sales team and account managers that their involvement is expected when necessary, begin to make them a regular report of past due accounts assigned to them. Do not inundate them, however, with each account that is past due and each billing and payment occurrence on the account. Cut them some slack. Only give them the worst, extreme accounts that may be a struggle, or even those sensitive, favored accounts that are delicate. Try to keep the request of their involvement rare and this will render a better result.

Value Based Management For Accounts Receivable

Once they are accepting of this and participating when they receive these collection reports, move on to the next step. Help them in return with their sales. Let them know that their help is appreciated and their time is valued greatly.

Paying Attention To The Needs Of The Sales Department

Traditionally speaking, sales departments and credit departments are as natural of enemies as cats and dogs. The sales clerk makes a sale but the credit department denies them credit. The sales clerk is trying to sweet talk a customer into giving him or her more of their business, but the credit and collections department has spoiled it with hard collection tactics. The sales person wants a $3,000 line of credit for their client but credit just reduced their line of credit to $500. Sales say yes, credit says no. That is the traditional scenario and this good cop, bad cop routine will not help the profit margin. Nevertheless, that scenario does not have to be reality, in fact, business will prosper if the credit policies are set up in such a way as to make best friends of the sales and credit/collections departments. Does this sound impossible? It is not.

Work to build synergy between the sales department and credit/collections department.

When it comes to the accounts receivable department, the sales force is the first aspect in that realm, not a separate one. The sales team goes out and finds those prospective new clients to whom the business will sell. What usually happens is a sales team goes out and sells to anyone and everyone just to make their quota. Then the credit department becomes their enemies because most of their new sales are denied credit. The collections department hates the sales department because they have the job of trying to get money off the "dead beats" (or so the collections department will say) the sales team sold. The sales department hates the credit and collections department because they cancel high commission orders the sales team just sold. If this all too familiar, then neither departments are being utilized correctly. Most credit policies are set to work against developing a cohesive relationship between sales and credit/collections. What is desired instead is a well-oiled machine, sales feeding into credit/collections and credit/collections feeding back into sales while building a synergy that utilizes the best resources of both to not only heighten sales but also bring the DSO to an all time low, and thus, make the profit margin high.

How is this done?

This is done by making the credit policies include that which is needed for the sales policies. In other words, the sales department does not have a set of policies separately written from the credit department policies. Administratively speaking, the sales department should be harbored under the credit department.

This is very unconventional, but it works.

To begin with, each sales clerk will be given a territory that can be easily accounted for in the accounts receivable system. For example, for a nitrous oxide distributor, then have sales clerks who concentrate on the medical industry, others who will concentrate on the welding industry and others who will concentrate on auto racing industry. Accounts receivables will be able to utilize the SIC codes of customers to separate those industries in their system. Another example of how to do this is, for example a commercial cleaning service, in this example the company can assign territories by zip codes or alphabetically. The accounts receivable department will be able to separate those categories as well.

The second to do is change how the sales clerks are paid. In most companies, a sales clerk is paid a small base salary and then earns a commission for every sale. From now on, the sales clerks do not earn a commission for every sale. The sales clerks will earn a commission for their accounts that they sold, that actually pay.

For example:

The Old Way: Salesperson Johnny sold a new account to the ABC Company. In addition to his base salary, Salesperson Johnny earns a commission for that new sale.

The New Way: Salesperson Johnny sold a new account to the ABC Company. In addition to his base salary, Salesperson Johnny gets nothing if the ABC Company does not pay their bills. When the ABC Company does pay their bill, then Salesperson Johnny gets his commission. The commission here will be represented in a manner reflecting more of a royalty off of the profit margin.

The beauty of this method is that it will make best friends out of the sales and credit/collections departments because it is the credit/collections team that will 'bring in the royalty' for the sales person. Whenever the collectors have a past due client who isn't paying, the salesperson assigned to that account will be the first to drive out to that customer to collect the money because it will be in their best interest to do so.

To best utilize this new concept the credit/collections departments should send out a standard report at regular intervals to the sales team letting them know which of their customers have not yet paid their bills on time. If the sales personnel want to earn their commissions, they will work with the collections department to help get those accounts paid.

Every business is different and the interworking labyrinth of business flow will mandate tweaking on how this synergy will be laid out. Even so, work toward building a cooperative synergy between the sales department and the credit/ collections department that will increase the profits.

Gaining Support

The Sales Department

Usually, the accounts receivable department is set to hound the customer until they pay their bills. Typically, this is why the sales department resists this behavior. Their job is to win over the customer and gain their business. They do that promising the moon and serving it them with a silver tray and 'yes' attitude. Credit and collections, by instinct will counter to that. They resist with caution what the sales department will bring to them next, asking the impossible.

The problem here is that there is no synergy between them. They are not sharing goals, they are not working towards the same end and they both have equal power.

Realize that if the customer does not pay their bills then it is useless to win their business. An account that does not pay does no good. Therefore, sales must bend towards the credit department when they have evidence that the prospect is a credit risk. For the same reason, understand that if credit had their way, everyone would be on C.O.D. terms. Therefore, credit must learn to to take a little risk as well.

Gaining cooperation from other departments for the receivables department is a valuable tool that is well worth the effort. It will take work and an adjustment to change by everyone involved in order to accomplish this. Allow receivables to make the first effort by giving to the other departments whatever they can to assist them first.

Geographically, it is also beneficial to bring the credit and sales departments physically close together. Let them share the same space so that they can hear and see each other throughout the workday. Sales Associate Johnny will hear the multitude of collections calls to the ABC Company and Receivables Associate Tommy will hear what accounts are priority to the sales team and how hard they are working to make those sales.

The Purchasing Department

Quite often, the purchasing department is in an entirely different area of the building from credit/collections and on a daily routine, they do not interact too often. When products are ordered, purchasing buys them and when inventory is low, purchasing buys the items with which to stock the warehouse or production lines. Credit does not interfere with purchasing directly; credit's concern is the sales department and what goes out of the building, not what comes in.

However, there is an opportunity here for purchasing to boost the effectiveness of credit and collections that is often overlooked. After all, it is purchasing that sees what is ordered to be sold to whom, they are the ones that can notice the red flags first and give a heads up to credit.

One such method is with items of direct drop ship when the company usually keeps the inventory needed on hand and drop ship is not the norm. Since drop ship items come directly from the original vendor and go straight to the customer these items are often high dollar items, as high dollar items are not often kept in stock, but ordered when needed. When such things arise, the purchasing department can send a report to the credit department alerting them what was ordered and by whom. This is necessary because it is not always the case that approval has been acquired before credit receives notification of the order.

A business that maintains its own warehouse keeps on hand those items which are mainstream stock. Purchasing should be sending a regular report to the credit team regarding ordering trends. This is important because certain items are more of a higher risk for nonpayment than others. For example, if the business is an office supply company then understand that technology items such as computers are a higher risk than copy paper. If the purchasing department has a rise in purchasing trends on high-risk items, then something is wrong and the credit department needs to be aware.

The Customer Service/Order Entry Department

The customer service department usually concentrates on orders and customer service issues. Their goal is to satisfy the customer, to extend excellent customer service. To do that, they must completely satisfy the customer with the concerns that prompted the call. One key element that should be put into place is to ensure that the customer service department maintains awareness of any past due balances when talking to the customer.   If the customer is calling to order 15 more large sheets of aluminum and they are 60 days past due on the last order of aluminum then customer service should address this past due balance.

Value Based Management For Accounts Receivable

There are other opportunities that occur in the customer service/data entry department that could be valuable indicators to the collections department.

Once such moment is requested invoices or requested purchase orders by the customer. When customers call to get copies of invoices or purchase orders, a lot of the time they reach the customer service desk to make those requests. The customer service department fulfills this request with a smile. Do they send word to the collections department that ABC Company just requested a copy of an invoice or purchase order? Should they? Yes, they should.

The request for a copy of a purchase order, and likewise an invoice, is an indication that something is amiss internally within the customer's company. They do not have all they need in place to begin the approval process to pay an invoice. Here is where the collections department can call them and ask if there is anything they can do to assist the customer, gain the information on what the delay is and get a feel on when the invoice will be paid in order to expedite the process. Much of the time it will be something as simple as they just need a copy of the invoice. However, if the same company calls often to request invoices, then there is an opportunity here to find out why they are not getting the invoices. Is the customer's business too large and therefore internal communications are not complete? Are the daily invoices into the customer inundating a single payables clerk who is overloaded? Are the invoices, upon mailing, being sorted and stuffed correctly? If the customer truly is not receiving the invoices repeatedly, the root cause is commonly associated with overburden in some way, either the personnel or machinery or both, but in some way or another.

Value Based Management For Accounts Receivable

Accounts Payable

One of the key departments that can be a very useful tool to credit/collections is the accounts payable department. Accounts payable controls the money that goes out. They pay the vendors and they also pay the customers for credits, returns and such. It is common for a company to buy from and sell to the same corporations. The accounts payable department needs to have a list of these companies that are both customers and vendors; they can send a report to the credit department of balances owed to these same companies for approval for payment. The reason for this is so that the credit department can call these companies and offer to offset balances. If the company owes $50 to ABC Corporation and ABC Corporation owes the company $100 then just have them pay $50. This offer to offset balances is a strong motivation in getting the customers to pay because it reduced the amount they have to shell out.

When a customer has returned a product and a credit is issued to their account, occasionally they will call to request a refund check. Those calls invariably will go to the accounts payable department. Before they issue any refund checks, they need to submit this to the credit department for approval first, because if that company or person still owes a balance, then payables should not be sending them out a refund check. Offer to offset their balance instead.

Your Employees

Department Heads

Who the company's managers are is just as important as the business type. It is not enough to simply have top-notch department heads who really know their stuff. It is very important that the department heads are personable, well liked individuals who know how to get along with employees and know how to make employees feel valuable, appreciated and knowledgeable. The most important tool to the company is the employees, the "front lines." The company can have department heads making the decisions that count, but unless the employees are there to carry out the daily tasks with skill and satisfaction, the company will not fly.

The managers have to know the job of their employees, know what they are doing and be smart. They have to be able to train without demeaning. They have to see the positive things about people and not the negative. They have to do what they say they will do. They have to listen. They have to know what is important to their crew and find the importance in it themselves. They have to put their departments first, ahead of their own goals.

Why is this being mentioned? How does this relate to the receivables and profit margin? The credit and collections department will always be the single most *mood delicate* department in the company. The mood of the receivables department reflects the attitude that is extended to the customer. The managers are responsible for setting that tone. Remember that it is the tone at the top that trickles down.

Walk into any large call center style collection agency and what will be seen are bright colors, balloons, photos of family, lively plants and team leaders walking around the floor assisting the crew. The team leaders will be positively motivating the staff and be ready to answer any question with knowledge and thoroughness that is raised to them. A call center collection agency would not function if the atmosphere of the business and attitude and knowledge of the managers reflected the negative aspect of the role.

Value Based Management For Accounts Receivable

An in-house, even a small business in-house collection team needs the same bestowment from their managers.

The Front Lines

The key aspects that make up the bottom line to any business are the front line employees and all that they do and touch. The company may have the world's most elite, stellar marketing and public relations team in the world promoting the image of the company all the while the CEO is out kissing babies and pulling cats down from trees, all in the name of company image, but in truth, none of that matters to the image the business' customers get of the company. The only thing that matters to the image the customers get of the company are the front line employees they talk to daily and how those employees treat them. How those employees treat the customer is in direct relation to how the managers treat the employees.

To give an example of how this might be employed, some of the savviest businesses retitle their Receptionist to Director of First Impressions. That is not just a tool to make the Receptionist feel important, it is an indication of what the company expects the Receptionist to do; make great first impressions on behalf of the company. Businesses that do this understand that the front line employees are the most valuable to company reputation. The company's reputation precedes the phone calls the collections department makes, a negative reputation is met with arguments against paying the invoice while a positive reputation is met with cooperative discussions in how to get the invoice paid.

The company's past due receivables really are affected by the working environment of the collections clerks. This is because they are whom the customers deal with. Allowing for an imagined scenario, envision that the accounts receivable clerk just had their stapler stolen from their desk for the

30th time, has just come back from lunch only to find that someone stole their fruit out of their lunch sack or took a bite of their sandwich, just read an email from H.R. stating their vacation days request was denied because an executive requested those days and they have to wait, now that they are back at their desk, they won't be in a good mood. Then they get on the phone to call XYZ Company regarding past due invoices. The accounts payable clerk from XYX Company is explaining the technical reasons that it is impossible to pay that invoice at this time. The accounts receivables clerk has had enough and lets the representative from XYZ Company know it. This is an example of how atmosphere in the work place affects the receivables. When the Sales Associate assigned to XYX Company makes their next sales call, most likely they won't be as warmly received as they could have been.

The accounts receivable clerk has a negative job; they are after all, a bill collector. They call the customers in order to collect on unpaid invoices. Regardless of how past due the invoice is, that invoice still belongs to the customer. The customer is the bread and butter of the company. What kind of an image should be portrayed to the customer during a phone call from the receivables department? It should be professional, courteous and upbeat. Therefore the working environment of the receivables team needs also to be professional, courteous and upbeat.

Treat the front line employees like gold. Make them happy to be there. That is not impossible to do. Usually, what stops a company from creating an atmosphere that allows hourly wage workers to feel good about who they are within a company are the executives themselves. The executives and managers in the company must recognize that times have changed and the most important person in that building is not the CFO but the clerks doing the dirty work. Any military general during wartime will state that the soldiers are the most important people in the unit fighting that war. A business is no different. In order to put into place a good atmosphere for the employees it is crucial to offer decent, fair and competitive wages. Possibly put into place some sort of profit sharing or performance bonus plan. Offer up-to-date furnishings for them to work at. Keep the building, break room and bathrooms clean and well stocked as well as cheerily decorated. Offer a lockable drawer or file cabinet or locker for the employees to store their valuables. Brighten the place up with color and lighting and green plants. Congratulate jobs well done often. Take time to talk to them about their families and offer a little flexibility in their schedules.

Look for every way possible to offer them financial benefits such as lower insurance rates, 401K matching, and increased PTO accrual.

Get To Know Them Personally

Most importantly, extend to them courtesy and respect. Build up trust with the employees. Communicate positively and openly. Respect their intelligence. Create a team environment with team building activities. Celebrate business and personal milestones in the office. Give recognition and appreciation. Give credit to them and take responsibility to the managers. Be approachable. Make the workplace fun.

Installing Incentives

What incentivizes an employee to do their job exceptionally? Certainly, the threat of termination will hold a good amount of incentive for that employee to perform, but only up to the adequate level, performing adequately keeps them from being fired but it does not create in them the exceptional performance level sought in employees. Running a credit and collections department requires exceptional employees because it requires the employee to exhaust their reasoning and sales skills in order to make the numbers above goal. It takes motivating them towards excellence. There is only one way to do this and that is by installing meaningful incentives. Begin searching for monetary incentives that can be put into place. The employee will earn their salary for doing their job, in fact, they will earn the same salary for adequate level work that they will for excellent work and excellent work being harder, where is the incentive to perform? There is none based on simply salary alone.

The first thing suggested to do is put in place performance measures and goals that explain what is expected from them as the minimum level performance, which will be above adequate. Like a quota, they must maintain this level not only to earn their salaries but also to keep their jobs. However, go above that and install incentives for goal achievement that places their performance at the excellent level. What goals should be put in place? That decision will be based on many factors such as the size of the company, its cash flow and desires of the employees. Some examples of what might be offered are bonuses, paid time off, catered lunches, outings or material prizes.

Incentives For Accounts Receivable

The best incentive to install for the accounts receivable department is a commission or bonus based on collected dollars. To offer them a bonus based incentive, assign them a goal and when they reach it, they receive a bonus. Most collectors like a commission incentive better, however, because in addition to their base salary, they receive a certain percentage of all the dollars they bring in; it makes their paycheck unlimited and it really does motivate them to collect.

There are other methods of installing incentives for the accounts receivable team however that do not include money. There is earned time off, catered lunches, special department outings, movies, gifts and trinkets, dress down days, food days and so forth. Sometimes the best incentive is simply recognition. Letting everyone know at the company meeting that Collector #1 really did an outstanding job that month and achieved 15% above his/her quota so that he/she can stand and receive applause is a very powerful incentive. Everyone wants to feel they have value and are appreciated.

Another great incentive is special projects. Those that are the top performing receivable clerks might get to perform special projects that take them away from the daily, mundane routine. The project can be anything, little or big, as long as it gives them something new and different to do away from their normal work routine for a while.

Another top motivating incentive is that the top performers get a few hours each week to act as department managers. They can assign shift duties; listen to phone calls for coaching purposes or any other such managerial function. This is also a good way to train future managers.

Another possible incentive is a department exchange. Everyone wants to move up in a company and the collectors are no exception to that rule. Work it out with the other department heads that they would receive the receivables top employees for a few hours each month to cross train them as a reward for doing a good job. The idea here is that they would train in a department they are interested in moving into, then when the job opportunities arise, they have a chance at the promotion.

Incentives For The Other Departments

The other departments such as accounts payable, purchasing, customer service and order entry will not be structured so that commission and bonus incentives are as easy to track as receivables. It is, however, still possible. Each department will have its own performance measures with which to use.

Even still, all the suggestions laid out for the accounts receivable department would fare just as well in the other departments. What is important here is that these additional incentives are geared to these other departments with the receivables in mind.

The various departments within the company are all linked together and they all serve the same purpose: to make the company a profit. The key department to ensuring the accounts are in the black is the accounts receivable department and all the other departments should extend assistance towards their goal.

Customer service and order entry personnel talk to the customer as well, they too can collect payments on current or past due orders. Do not limit the bonus or commission for collecting funds to the accounts receivable department. If the customer service rep collects funds for a past due invoice during a servicing call, pay them their dues.

All the departments, from purchasing to sales and the entire crew, have work details that affect receivables. Within every one of those tasks is an opportunity to aid the collectors. Those are the opportunities to look for to encourage with incentives.

However, it is not all about the accounts receivable department. The top paid people in the company need to be the sales team. Without sales, the business has no company. Once the sale is made however, every other thing the employees do, they do with the end goal in mind of getting the customer to pay for their order or service they have received.

Value Based Management For Accounts Receivable

What are some examples of opportunities that lie within other departments to aid receivables? How can they be identified? Look for process improvement opportunities. As an example, suppose the Retro-Cool Corp often orders from the company; this time, however, they have notified the company that only Joe, Karen and Pat are authorized to order. What happens if Sam places and order for the Retro-Cool Corp? The invoice will not be paid, that is what happens. Another example is Grinding-Monkey Inc orders a specialized custom-made part out of pre-fab metal, only the company's purchasing department ordered the wrong metal to use for the part. Grinding-Monkey will not accept the shipment and the sale has just been lost. Walking Fish LLC just placed an order and the purchase order taken for the order is either missing or incorrect. Nothing irritates the accounts receivable department more than a missing or incorrect purchase order numbers. It makes it very difficult to collect payment, sometimes impossible. These are the opportunities that the other departments can do to aid the accounts receivable department.

Check For Work Accuracy

Preventing problems is the key to preventing payment delays. Just like a student getting ready to turn in his/her math homework, the company too must check their work. Do that by trying to guess what excuses and problems will come up on each file, on each customer and on each sale that would prevent the company from being paid. This is a very effective way to eliminate problems before they happen.

To do this, try playing a game called 'pretend to be them'; the point of this game is to put the company in the customer's shoes and try to come up with an effective way to avoid paying the invoice other than ' I have no money'. Open the pending invoices and corresponding sales files and choose a customer or sale. Go over the transaction from start to finish as well as the customer's account data file. Try to come up with a viable reason to avoid paying the invoice. The game simply reflects what an auditor or quality control person would do, it is adjusted to "find a reason not to pay" and in this way the smaller details tend to be easier to find.

For example, what might be derived is:

- There is no purchase order number on the ticket.
- No proof of delivery was provided.
- The purchase order allotment was exceeded on this invoice.
- The purchaser was not an authorized buyer for the company.
- The wrong part number was provided.
- The amount billed does not match the quote.
- The deadline for job completion was exceeded.
- The wrong address and/or method was used.
- There is an open, unused credit on the customer's account.

There are a myriad of reasons that might discovered. Nevertheless, playing this game every now and then will give the company an understanding of where the holes are and where the company needs to improve things in order to improve receivables.

Good Practices To Put Into Place

Notate everything! Whenever an account is pulled up by anyone in the office, make sure every detail of when and why is notated. Even if the account is pulled up just to verify the address, notate that. Even if the account is pulled up just to look at it, notate that, "reviewed account." Every essence of everything done must be notated in the account. Most certainly, this goes for conversations and communications with the customer. Notate who, when, how, why and what for each occasion. Understand the value of notating when the customer called and what was said. These are windows into the account; most software will keep track of payment histories and invoice histories and such, but other histories on the account are up to the user to document. The "picture" of the account can be seen in the notations made throughout its history.

—————

Do not ever use the phrase "may result in . . ." on any communication to the customer. Most of the time when a company threatens with "may result in...." they want to put fear in the customer by making them think bad things are going to happen if they don't comply with the request, however the truth is the company very rarely has any intentions of following through with these threats and the customer knows it. "May result in..." does not affect the motivation it is intended.

—————

Follow through on intentions. If something is communicated to the customer that the company is going to do something, then do it in exactly the method of when and how it was conveyed.   The only thing that will get the customers to comply with the rules is if they know the company is serious. It is the same thing as when a child hears his or her parent say, "If you don't pick up your toys I'll sit you in the corner" and an hour later the toys are still on the floor and the child is still running around playing happily.

—————

Do not use mediators to settle legal disputes. Mediators take away the court privileges by limiting all parties to certain actions. Everyone have a right to full court judicial treatment and even a corporation wants to make sure they get it.

It is common for a mediator to play favorites, especially one hired and commonly used by the other people. This is why corporations use mediators so often, they tend to be biased towards the ones who have initiated the long term contract of their use. Even so, they are not the wisest of methods in deciding judicial matters.

———————

Consider sending invoices on the 15th as most companies pay bills on 25th.

———————

Check the paper trail. Is there enough evidence to support the company's claims? Pretend to be the customer and try to come up with an excuse not to pay the invoice. This needs done regularly by someone in the office who is very detail oriented and a proactive thinking.

———————

Negotiations and settlements are good things. It is ok to not be fully paid if the company truly is facing the reality of not being paid at all. Negotiate away!

———————

Ensure there is a "No Modification Clause in place. When backed up against a wall, a debtor will often claim that they were promised extended payment terms, a waiver of interest or additional services or merchandise, or some other change from the agreement currently held with the customer. That is where a 'no modification' provision comes in. As long as the company can point to a provision in the agreement that invalidates any modification of the agreement except those made in writing and signed by both parties, the debtor's argument is null.

———————

Make sure to keep all emotions in check. This is going to be very hard to do in this genre of business, but it is imperative and it really does make the difference between a good executive and a poor one as well as a good receivables professional and a poor one. The company cannot make the right business decisions that maximizes profit if emotions are not in check. For example, a medium sized manufacturer, we will call "Bob's Business," went severely default. Bob's Business went default with a lot of creditors; basically all of his creditors, actually. He went into the red and had nothing to offer anyone in way of repayment. It wasn't intentional on his part, just bad management combined with a bad economy and a lot of customers of Bob's going under as well. Despite his best efforts and intentions however, when Bob's creditors began to call him, his attitude turned defensive. He came across as someone who did not care about his debt and that angered a lot of people. One creditor had a conversation with him that went like this:

"Hello Bob, this is Kim your creditor, I'm calling about the $45,000.00 past due balance you owe us. Can you pay that in full today or do you need a payment plan?"

"No," Bob said, "don't got money. Good luck getting your money." He said, and with that he hung up. This was the 12th call of the day that poor Bob had went through by this time and many of the previous creditors who called used hard ball tactics, really putting Bob on the defensive.

The creditor did not bother to call him back. Instead the creditor looked for other avenues to collect their funds, and performed an asset search. It was discovered that Bob truly was devoid of anything of value. He'd already sold off everything he could and did the best he could to recover; however he failed. That was it for Bob.

About a month or so later this creditor was contacted by a representative of ABC Law firm, we'll call James Jackson, Attorney. Mr. Jackson represented the majority of Bob's creditors. They got together and hired Mr. Jackson in order to form a joint lawsuit against Bob's Business with the aim and purpose of forcing Bob into bankruptcy. Mr. Jackson wanted to persuade the creditor to join in the lawsuit against Bob.

The creditor asked Mr. Jackson why he and the other parties to the suit thought this was a good idea. Mr. Jackson explained that Bob's unpaid debt was severely hurting his creditors and it was time to take effective action in getting the matter resolved.

The creditor asked Mr. Jackson, how forcing Bob into bankruptcy was going to do that. In a Chapter 13, Mr. Jackson explained, Bob's assets will be liquidated and disbursed to his creditors.

What if he doesn't file a Chapter 13? The creditor wanted to know, what if he files a Chapter 7 and receives full protection from obligation to all his debt. Mr. Jackson then went into a lengthy legal explanation at how the judicial system worked in a situation like this and just how it was that the end result was going to be a Chapter 13 for Bob's Business. The creditor wasn't able to debate with Mr. Jackson on legal terms, not being certain if the answer Mr. Jackson provided was true or not, the credit assumed its truth for the sake of the discussion and asked Mr. Jackson how the chapter 13 would benefit the plaintiffs if there were no assets to liquidate and disperse. Mr. Jackson explained, even if there were no assets to liquidate, the lawsuit would put the creditors named as party to the suit in the front of the line to be paid first, before anyone else, collateral or not, when and if there was money to dole out. In other words, they wanted certainty that at some point, Bob would pay them, willingly or unwillingly.

The creditor pointed out to Mr. Jackson that a UCC filing would do the same thing. While Mr. Jackson did explain the legal ramifications of a UCC filing versus a court suit for bankruptcy, even still, the conversation didn't go much farther. The credit stated firmly he did not want to be party to the suit.

One by one, over the next week or two, this creditor who refused to join the suit began to receive phone calls from the other creditor participants in the lawsuit, all of whom tried to persuade this single creditor to take part. The credit held firm, no.

The creditor's reasons for not wanting to take part, was that Bob was Desolate with a capital D. If bankruptcy, for whatever reason, was not an option chosen by Bob himself then there just didn't seem to be any reason to force Bob into filing bankruptcy.

This is where the real reasons behind the lawsuit came out. One by one, they all commented on how awful a person Bob was to take advantage of them, how criminal it was that he stole from them, they complained at how rude he was on the phone. Bob was just a jerk, they said, and he deserves what he gets when this lawsuit comes out. In other words, they just wanted revenge. They wanted to put Bob in his place for "hurting" them. It was an emotional response and that was all.

Not only was it an emotional response, it was not a very sound business decision. The money it cost them to engage in the lawsuit was never paid to the attorneys because Bob simply didn't have the money. Bob was forced into bankruptcy and they never saw a dime of payment because Bob filed a Chapter

7. Maybe Mr. Jackson was wrong, or maybe Bob had a better attorney, it doesn't matter because the suit did no good for the other creditors.

One year later Bob met a man who owned a large manufacturing business who liked Bob's business experience and gave him a job running a new branch of his factory. Yes, Bob had a failed business, but he still had the know how to run a factory. In his new position, when it came time to purchase materials, Bob called that single creditor who refused to take part in the law suit. Bob said that he remembered how the creditor tried to work with him when Bob's Business was down and out and falling faster and he appreciated that the creditor didn't join the party who forced him into bankruptcy. Bob opened a credit account with this same creditor for his employer's company. The relationship grew. The account became a long standing, good account that proved very profitable. Despite the write-off of Bob's Business debt, in the end, thinking without emotion enabled the creditor to make the right decision which led to profitable gains in the end.

Certainly this example is not typical by any means. It is only meant to demonstrate that in the business of accounts receivable, emotion has not business at all.

CHAPTER SIX – The FDCPA & The Consumer Debtor

The Fair Debt Collections Practices, known as FDCPA, act is the most important piece of legislature affecting the credit and collections industry; it is the Bible of accounts receivable. The FDCPA was not always around, it came into being in 1978 and is here to stay; it will not go away or become more lenient, if anything, it will become stricter. Adherence to the FDCPA is not an option, whether the company is a third or first party collector, the company still needs to adhere to the tight controls of the FDCPA.

Know also that each state also has their own versions of the FDCPA and each state maintains and regulates their own rules regarding debt collections and credit. It is not enough to know the Federal laws regarding credit and collections, the company must also know the state laws for each state it conduct business. Chapter six of this text only deals with Federal regulations, it is up to each company to familiarize themselves with the applicable state regulations.

Communication With Consumers And Third Parties

The FDCPA limits communications regarding the debt owed to only the person owing the debt and his or her legally married spouse. This can be a bit tricky, because the courts do recognize common law marriages in dealing with the rights of either spouse in certain situations; however in this situation common law marriage is not a legal form of marriage for revealing consumer debt to another individual other than the debt holder. Essentially, here, consider a legal marriage to be one that would require a legal court divorce in order to dissolve the marriage. Also, know that gender plays no part in the definition of legal marriage for the purposes of the FDCPA. If two same sex individuals were legally married in their state then they are legally married and the company as the collector or creditor is bound to honor that, even if the company is in a state that disallows same sex marriages.

The most common mistake made regarding this is when the debt collector leaves a message. The customer might hear a home voice mail message identifying Mr. And Mrs. Smith and the debtor is Mr. Smith, so they leave a message something like this, "Mr. Smith please call ABC Debt Collections Company regarding your bill that was due June 31st." That is a violation of the FDCPA because it is not known who will over hear that message. If that message is overheard by the neighbor Mr. Johnson because they were in the Smith's home when it was played, that is the company's liability not Mr. Smith's for the revelation of Mr. Smith's private business. The company cannot state anything in a voice mail message that would allude to why they are calling who they are. In that situation it is recommended something like, "Mr. Smith please call 1800 555 5555 regarding an important business matter, this is not a sales call. Thank you." Or perhaps, "This call is for Mr. Smith regarding a personal business matter, please call 1800 555 5555. Thank you."

Another thing that happens very frequently and gets many debt collectors in trouble is the aging debtor scenario. The collector calls for Mrs. Smith because Mrs. Smith is past due on a bill, so the collector dials the residential phone number and the line is answered. The collector asks for Mrs. Smith and the person who answered asks who is calling.

"This is Mike Johnson of the ABC Company, I'm calling on a personal business matter." The collector says.

"Can you tell me what this is about, this is Sheila Connors, Mrs. Smith is my mother." They say.

"I'm Sorry Mrs. Connors, I'm not able to discuss the matter with you, I am only authorized to talk to Mrs. Smith."

"Well my mother Mrs. Smith is old and sick and isn't able to discuss anything with you, if you want this matter dealt with you'll have to talk to me."

"I'm sorry Mrs. Connors, I understand your frustration but Federal regulations forbid me to discuss the matter with anyone but Mrs. Smith without her permission. If she is there to give me permission to discuss this with you, I'd be glad to talk to you about it."

"Well, I'll put my mother on the line, but she has Alzheimer's so I doubt she'll understand you."

Okay, there is the problem. The caller has just been told that Mrs. Smith is not of her right mind, the caller has been told that Mrs. Smith has Alzheimer's. Most debt collectors would get Mrs. Smith on the phone and stumble through getting her to say that it is okay to talk to her daughter Sheila Connors, and then they talk to Sheila Connors revealing Mrs. Smith's debt. That is a violation of the FDCPA. Mrs. Smith must be of sound mind and body and must knowingly and without coercion give permission to discuss the matter with her daughter. Permission given under any other circumstance is in violation of Federal law. In this scenario, the only thing that can be done is tell Sheila Connors that she will have to fax or send via certified mail a copy of a court granted power of attorney giving her legal right to deal with her mother's affairs. Until that happens, only send the matter of the debt to Mrs. Smith via mail addressed to her and only her.

Another scenario that causes problems is when the debt collector called by an attorney saying they represent Mrs. Smith and request the details of the debt. Mrs. Smith must still give permission to discuss the matter with her attorney, or Sheila Connors must give the permission if she has provided a power of attorney. Do not be pressured by the attorney to reveal the debt, if they are a good attorney they will understand and respect the desire to protect their client's privacy. Once permission has been obtained to discuss matters with their attorney, matters must dealt with their attorney only and cease contact with the debtor unless otherwise granted permission.

Be careful as well of seniors and juniors. A collector might call for Edward Anderson and the man who answers says he is Edward Anderson, however the caller needed Edward Anderson Jr. and who was reached was Sr.; verify whom is speaking on the line.

Time And Place Of Contact

Collections calls can only be placed between the hours of 8:00 AM and 8:00 PM in their own time zone unless he local province, county or state deems differently, and some do. Be very careful of that, it is quite easy to forget to check the time zone and allowable calling times of the debtor before calling, especially when only a few hundred miles separates the caller and called. Another thing to watch is the states that do not follow daylight savings time.

It is legal to call on Saturdays and in some states, it is legal to call on Sundays. Be aware of the state's regulations, because most states forbid calls on Sundays.

Contacting The Debtor On The Job

There are several types of business that do not allow employees to take or make personal calls during working hours. Factories are one such example, medical facilities, schools and call centers others. If it is known that the place of business for the debtor does not allow personal phone calls then do not call their place of business and ask to speak to them, instead contact human resources or a published employee message line and leave a nondescript and generic message for the debtor to call back on their break.

If the debtor instructs they do not desire to be contacted at work, then contacts at work should cease.

Do not send debt collection mail to the debtors job because it will be opened by a receptionist or mailroom clerk before it reaches them.

Ceasing Communications

If the debtor advises by written notice that they do not want to receive any further collection efforts, then the company may not communicate with the debtor any further except to advise them that the company is going to pursue legal proceedings or other special remedies outside of the norm that will affect them in some legal way. It is imperative they are forewarned of legal intent but always do this through legal counsel.

Harassment And Abuse

The FDCPA prohibits, directly, any form of:

- Verbal Abuse
- Threats of Violence or Unrealistic Consequences
- Empty Threats of Legal Suits
- Obscene Language
- Name Calling or Other Verbal Intimidation Tactics
- Publishing or Making Public In Any Way Their Private Debt or Threatening To Do So
- Repeating Telephone Calls (Call & Leave A Message No More Than Once Every Three Business Days)
- Calling Them Without Identifying Oneself As A Debt Collector Trying To Collect A Debt
- Non-Use Of The Mini-Miranda
- Certain Inquiries That Have Nothing To Do With The Debt
- Leaving A Revealing Message That Reveals They Owe A Debt
- False or Misleading Representation (Making Them Believe Something That Isn't True)
- Collecting Debts Expired Beyond Its Statute Of Limitations
- Use of the words "Plaintiff" or "Defendant" or Any Other Terminology That Causes Them To Think There Is A Court Case When There Isn't
- Giving False Information About Their Credit

- Using Any Terminology, Written or Verbal, That Alludes The Debt Is Being Collected By A Government Agency or Attorney or Court When It Isn't
- Not Stating the Mini-Miranda At The Beginning Of All Communications, Written or Verbal: This is an attempt to collect a debt, any information gained will be used for that purpose.
- Changing Names: The FDCPA allows debt collectors to use a pseudonym for their protection when making collections calls, however whatever name is chosen to be used must be used consistently and always.
- Collection Of Additional Charges When They Weren't Previously and Expressly Made Aware Of Before The Debt Was Incurred
- Cashing Post Dated Checks Before The Check's Date
- Charging The Debtor For The Collection Call or Written Correspondence
- Use of Post Cards for Debt Collections
- Envelopes That Reveal The Nature of the Correspondence

Pursuing Legal Actions

Do so through a licensed attorney practiced in consumer debt laws. It is recommended that hiring an outside firm is always better than inside counsel.

If the business is selling to a consumer, the responsibility remains to that business to ensure that all dealings are within federal and state as well as local legalities. The term "buyers beware" really was for the good old' western days when the greatest American transportation system was the steam locomotive and indoor plumbing did not exist yet for most rural homes. Over the course of U.S. history, government has slowly put into place many pieces of consumer protection laws and has spent the decades building upon them in order to protect the consumer from dishonest business practices. This is a good thing. It is also something for the business to take very seriously. Even if the business does not deal directly with the consumer, it is strongly advisable to familiarize itself with the laws protecting consumers because there are so many overlapping gray areas in business today that it takes legal practical understanding as well as business savvy to run a profitable business today.

Regarding Exemptions

What is an exemption? An exemption means that essential property purchased by the consumer may not be taken away from the consumer before proper legal allowances on the part of the seller have been put into place to allow such repossession for lack of payment. In other words, if they do not pay for the items they purchased, the company cannot just go get those items back. The key here is that the business cannot threaten to repossess those items either. This is a very tricky pitfall, because while the business cannot threaten repossession, it can say unpaid accounts for merchandise will result in "steps one, two and three" which may in some cases lead to the legal repossession of the unpaid property, for example.

The Fair Debt Collections Practices Act provides in Section 807, Subdivision 5, that: "...a debt collector may not use any false, deceptive or misleading representations or means in connection with the collection of any debt. Without limiting the general application of the foregoing, the following conduct is a violation of this debt . . . the threat to take any action that cannot legally be taken or that is not intended to be taken."

Therefore, the creditor cannot threaten in any way to take away the buyer's exempt property. Be aware that this not only includes things purchased by the customers but it also includes wages and other compensation paid to the employees for work already performed. This is mentioned this because it is not uncommon for an employer to allow employees to purchase business inventory on credit and then threaten to withhold payroll from that employee if they do not pay for the goods. The employer cannot deduct the employee's paycheck without prior written consent of the employee for the payment of those goods.

The difficulty here is that it is very easy for a collection associate calling to collect a debt from a consumer to misspeak the wrong words and end up in legal trouble. Here is an example of a typical conversation that may occur on the phone between a debt collector and a consumer, on the surface, it seems like a natural conversation.

Debt Collector: "Mr. Anderson, please."

Consumer: "This is Mr. Anderson."

Debt Collector: "Mr. Anderson, this is Bob with XYZ Furniture Company, this is an attempt to collect a debt and any information gained will be used for that purpose. I am calling because our records indicate that your account with us is three months past due in the amount of $1500. Can you make that payment with me today on the phone?"

Consumer: "No because I'm not three months behind. I made a double payment to you folks last time I paid."

Debt Collector: "I understand, Mr. Anderson. However, the last conversation we had on June 3rd you agreed that at that time your account was three months behind, and at that time you promised to bring your account current. You only made two months payment at that time, so at that time you were still one month behind. We did not receive another payment from you and now we are into another billing cycle and you are again three months behind. I need you to bring your account current, Mr. Anderson."

Consumer: "I was let go from my job, I was denied unemployment compensation because of the terms of my termination and my wife doesn't work and our savings has been depleted. I have no cash and no income to pay you with at this time. I will do the best I can, I am looking for work and I have had interviews. If you can hold off a couple more weeks, I'm sure I'll have a job and can begin making payments again."

Debt Collector: "Mr. Anderson, I'm very sorry to hear of your recent bad luck. I do hope things begin to look up for you. While I'm certain your intentions are good, I do need to show a payment on the books in order to prevent the account from going over three months past due, and I need to post at least two payments today with you on the phone."

Consumer: "Well I can't pay you. What happens if the account goes past three months due?"

Debt Collector: "We initiate repossession Mr. Anderson."

Consumer: "Are you telling me, that if I don't give you two months payment today on the phone with you now, that you'll come into my home, take away my couches, chairs, tables and bedroom set? Leave my already overly worried and stressed wife to sit and sleep on the cold floor? You would do that to a man? You'd put a man already down on the ground?"

Debt Collector: "Mr. Anderson, I don't want to see that happen. However, our policies here are set and I am afraid I'll have no choice but to initiate repossession at the start of four months past due."

Value Based Management For Accounts Receivable

The rest of the conversation is subjective. Mr. Anderson can either choose to pay or he can choose to not pay, that is not the point. The point is that the debt collector has violated the FDCPA in this above conversation because he has alluded to and therefore threatened to repossess Mr. Anderson's furniture. Here is the way the conversation should have gone.

Debt Collector: "Mr. Anderson, please."

Consumer: "This is Mr. Anderson."

Debt Collector: "Mr. Anderson, this is Bob with XYZ Furniture Company, this is an attempt to collect a debt and any information gained will be used for that purpose. I am calling because our records indicate that your account with us is three months past due in the amount of $1500. Can you make that payment with me today on the phone?"

Consumer: "No because I'm not three months behind. I made a double payment to you folks last time I paid."

Debt Collector: "I understand, Mr. Anderson. However, the last conversation we had on June 3rd you agreed that at that time your account was three months behind, and at that time you promised to bring your account current. You only made two months payment at that time, so at that time you were still one month behind. We did not receive another payment from you and now we are into another billing cycle and you are again three months behind. I need you to bring your account current, Mr. Anderson."

Consumer: "I was let go from my job, I was denied unemployment compensation because of the terms of my termination and my wife doesn't work and our savings has been depleted. I have no cash and no income to pay you with at this time. I will do the best I can, I am looking for work and I have had interviews. If you can hold off a couple more weeks, I'm sure I'll have a job and can begin making payments again."

Debt Collector: "Mr. Anderson, I'm very sorry to hear of your recent bad luck. I do hope things begin to look up for you. While I'm certain your intentions are good, I do need to show a payment on the books in order to prevent the account from going over three months past due, and I need to post at least two payments today with you on the phone."

Consumer: "Well I can't pay you. What happens if the account goes past three months due?"

Debt Collector: "When an account shows more than three months of missed payments it is reviewed for further action. I want to prevent the account from reaching that stage, Mr. Anderson, and give you time to get some income coming in. Can you make one payment with me today and we'll take this one month at a time until you find work?"

Consumer: "No. I told you I do not have any money. I am being real with you on that. What kind of further action? What will happen?"

Debt Collector: "Any account reviewed for further action is done so by management under the advice of legal counsel and at that time I will be no longer involved. I can overnight you a letter from our legal advisor that will explain available options to you and your rights under the FDCPA. When you receive that letter, Mr. Anderson, please open it right away and call me back. Do I have your address correct? 123 Main Street?"

Consumer: "Yes that is correct. Send the letter, I'll take a look at it."

Value Based Management For Accounts Receivable

The difference between the first conversation and the second conversation is that in the second one, Mr. Anderson was not threatened with repossession. While the debt collector mentioned the words legal counsel he did not threaten any legal action to Mr. Anderson. The letter that will be received by Mr. Anderson will outline the available and allowable remedies to XYZ Furniture Company and clearly state the company's policies and their intended actions giving Mr. Anderson time to resolve the issue before the 'further actions' can take place.

Most retailers who deal with consumers on credit terms will have a collections policy set forth that takes further action after ninety days. What usually occurs is after three months of missed payments the consumer will receive a letter giving them so many days to pay on their account. If no payment is received within that period, the collector hits a few keys on their computer and the account goes into "advanced collections" which means that all the legal procedures are followed to initiate repossession. The business can repossess if it is done correctly, affording the consumer their due rights in the matter. Most collectors, however, don't think of the big picture, all they know is that they have done their best, worked hard to collect the past due amounts on the account, and now not having been able to, they 'send the account for repossession' by forwarding it for review of further action. The debt collector needs to think of this step as 'taking further action' not 'initiating repossession' even though it is realized that will be the final result, because the FDCPA clearly refutes the legalities of repossession without undue authorization. At the time the collector pushes those keys to begin the process, no authorization has been granted to repossess, therefore, that is not what is happening; all that is happening is the account is being reviewed for further action.

Pursuing Garnishments

Other than repossession, a creditor might choose another course of action when faced with the challenges of an uncollectable consumer credit account. Where applicable, another course of action is to pursue garnishment, which means the money is obtained from the consumer via their payroll or bank accounts, withheld from them and sent to the creditor via the court systems.

There are many businesses and debt collection agencies that are very well versed in the ramifications and legal procedures in obtaining a judgment for garnishment, and while they are knowledgeable enough to pursue this course of action for themselves, it is highly recommended that taking these steps are only done through legal counsel.

If the business is granted a legal judgment to pursue garnishment by the courts, even if the business uses legal counsel to handle the matter, they need to be aware that not all sources of monetary units are allowed to be garnished. Here are some restrictions:

Payroll and salaries can only be garnished up to a certain percentage. This amount varies from state to state.

Retirement and Pension incomes are exempt under the Employee Retirement Income Securities Act (E.R.I.S.A.)29 USC 1056(D).

Veterans benefits are also exempt under 38 USC 407 (A).

Social Security payments are exempt under 42 USC 407 (A).

Civil Service Retirement Benefits are exempt under 5 UFSC 8346 (A).

Railroad Retirement Act annuities and pensions are exempt under 45 USC Section 231 Subdivision M (A).

Payments under Longshoreman and Harbor Workers Compensation Act 33 USC 916 are exempt.

Alimony and child support payments are exempt.

Disability benefits are exempt.

Federal Financial Aid and Grants are exempt.

Insurance payments and contributions are exempt.

Welfare benefits are exempt.

Unemployment benefits are exempt.
Worker's compensation payments are exempt.

There are a lot of situations where garnishments would not be permissible. Even the amounts in bank accounts that are not protected by any of the above can be limited in percentage due to the holding names on the accounts. For example, if Charles A. Smith owed $5,000 and the courts granted judgment of garnishment against Charles A. Smith in favor of the creditor then that creditor can then attempt to garnish Charles A. Smith's monies for the amount owed of

$5,000. Now let us say that Charles A. Smith has a savings account for $8,000 whose deposits are not exempt, however the account also has the name of Rachel. R. Roberts. The creditor cannot garnish the full $5,000 from that account, even though there are enough funds and even though the deposits are not exempt because Rachel R. Roberts is co-owner of those funds and no judgment was granted against her, the debt not being hers.

Consumer Credit Contracts

Part of the purpose of the FDCPA is to protect the consumer against certain contract provisions that the government asserts to be unfair and possibly harmful to consumers. The contract regulations set forth by the FDCPA greatly restrict and limit the power of the creditor, however they are very necessary. What might seem like common sense today was not necessarily an action put into practice before the FDCPA. For example, contracts are required to clearly, explicitly and completely outline all obligations and risk to co-signers according to the rules of the FDCPA, which set this provision because contracts did not always outline these responsibilities. Another example is that creditors would vaguely describe late fee amounts due and other fees that might be assessed, then they would hit the consumer with the highest possible amount of fees as often as they could, being unrealized income, this was icing on the cake. The FDCPA put a stop to that and fees are specific, restricted and guided in frequency.

The most common things found in contracts previously, that were of great benefit to creditors, now blocked by the FDCPA are things that the company employees need to be aware of. Such as:

Confession of Judgment - Part of the "small print" at the bottom of a contract would contain what was called a confession of judgment, which granted the creditor an automatic judgment, meaning they would garnish the creditor automatically if no payments were received. The problem with this is that they would garnish after just one late payment, tack on large amount of "garnishment processing fees" and there was no warning to the consumer their monies would be absconded.

Waiver of Exemption – More "small print" detailing listed waivers of exemptions, which meant that the consumer waived all their exemption rights. No monies or funds, regardless of their source, were exempt from garnishments. Repossessions could happen without warning.

Assignment of Wages – The fine print of contracts also expressed the right of the creditor to assignment of wages. This meant that if the consumer failed to make a payment, the creditor had the right to arrange with the consumer's employer to withhold monies from the consumer's paycheck and send those monies straight to the creditor without warning or notice to the consumer.

Security Agreement - Household Goods - This was a very interesting fine print addendum. In this provision, creditors had the right to use any household goods the consumer owned, such as electronics, jewelry, appliances or anything of value as security and collateral for the credit debt. When a consumer missed a payment, repossession of the item would occur but it might also be that other household goods that were held in collateral due to this provision were confiscated instead. Therefore, Joe would miss his payment on his new chain saw, which he lent to his brother-in-law in Wisconsin, so the chain saw creditor might come and confiscate Joe Junior's new gaming unit.

Late Fees - One common practice that the FDCPA put an end to under the regulations for contract provisions was pyramiding of late charges. Pyramiding of late charges occurred when one payment was made after its due date and a late fee was assessed, but not paid promptly. All future payments were then considered delinquent even though they were paid in full within the required time period. As a result, late fees were assessed on all future payments.

The Retired Consumer

The FDCPA does not allow social security, retirement or other pensions to be garnished. There was a day long ago, unbelievably, when most people retired and lived off of their social security. Today, that is not possible. Today people need other sources of retirement income such as employer sponsored pension plans. Even with a second source of income added to their monthly social security check, it is sometimes difficult for the retired person to make ends meet. The retired person is allowed to seek part-time employment or other income from, for example, contracted or consulting work. They might make and sell products out of their garage. Whatever they do, they can continue to earn monies while earning retirement pay and while the company cannot garnish their retirement pay, the company can garnish their other sources of income.

Another tip is that many retirement persons while working all their lives, put away a "nest egg." That is, they would stash away money into a bank savings account. Even though a person is retired, even if they are living only on retirement benefits, any monies sitting in a bank account that was put there from regular payroll during their working years the company can garnish. This is mentioned not as an encouragement to go out and deplete retired persons of their money, but it is mentioned because a creditor sometimes can fall victim to credit abuse, even by a retired person.

Credit to Minors

Basically, do not do it. Minors have the right to back out of any contract they enter into and a creditor cannot hold them liable to make good on payments. Parents are legally responsible for the necessities of the child such as food, clothing, shelter, educational costs, medical costs and other pertinent care costs. Parents are not obligated to pay for luxury items such as video games, bicycles, and sporting equipment even for team sports, video or music materials.

If the business markets things for children, do not sell to children, only to the adult responsible for them. If the business does so, then here is a typical example of a conversation that business might end up having:

Business: "May I speak to Johnny Johnstone?"

Consumer: "This is Mrs. Johnstone, Johnny is a minor and my son. To whom am I speaking?"

Business: "This is Jane Smith, I'm with the Gadgets Corporation. Is Johnny available?"

Consumer: "No. You may speak to me, as I said, he is a minor and I am his parent. What is this about?"

Business: "Mrs. Johnstone, this is Jane Smith with the Gadgets Corporation. Johnny ordered "Martian Stone Zombies" video game for the PC from us, which was shipped, and we have not received payment. I'm looking for $49.95 + tax in payment."

Consumer: "I see. Well, I remember Johnny receiving this video game, and I asked him where he got it, he said that he had ordered it. He said that he saw a commercial on television for the game, called the 800 number and ordered the game. I asked him at that time, if he had paid for the game and where did he get the money. He said he did not pay for it, he just called and gave his address and they shipped it to him. I do not think he understood that this was something that was a billable item. I think he thought it was free."

Business: "I understand Johnny might have been confused, however we do sell this item at a cost of $49.95, which is now past due. We take Visa and MasterCard as well as check by phone. How will you be paying for this item?"

Consumer: "I'm not going to."

Business: "Oh, I understand. You want Johnny to pay for it. So he learns his lesson huh? I get it. I got kids too. Ok. Put Johnny on the phone, I will collect from him. Would you like him to be lectured on not ordering things without permission?"

Consumer: "Excuse me? Listen, I already told you I am not putting Johnny on the phone, because he is a minor, I am his parent and you are not permitted to speak to him. Do not call this number again and do not ask for Johnny. Is that clear Miss Jane Smith?"

Business:"I am sorry Mrs. Johnstone, I must have misunderstood you. When you said you were not paying for it, I thought you wanted Johnny to pay for it. That is fine. I apologize for the misunderstanding. Do you prefer to mail in your payment?"

Consumer: "No. I am not paying for it. I told you that already. Do you understand me now?"

Business: "Mrs. Johnstone, Johnny ordered this product from us, you acknowledged that he did receive it. We have not received payment. This item must be paid for and I must insist you pay for the item Johnny ordered. He is your child after all."

Consumer: "Now you listen to me Jane Smith. I do not know where you are or where you come from, maybe you are calling from another country or perhaps you hail from Mars yourself, because if you were from this country you would know that minors cannot enter into a contract and be held accountable for that contract. Buying an item over the phone from one of your television commercials is a type of verbal contract, Johnny is a minor, therefore you cannot make him pay for that video game nor am I paying for it. Do you understand?"

Business: "Mrs. Johnstone, my company will send any past due account that is past due over 120 days to a collection agency. Do you want that?"

Consumer: "Jane Smith, you and the Gadget Company must be the dumbest people on Earth. I strongly advise you do not attempt to notify any collection agency of this matter or you will be sued in court, and you will lose. I also strongly advise you not to sell things to minors if you expect to get paid. Have you ever heard of the FDCPA? I advise you to learn it."

And that would be the end of that call and the end of the matter.

CHAPTER SEVEN - Skip Tracing – Finding the Consumer Debtor or Failed Business Owner

Websites

There are several websites that offers skip tracing services for a fee, a lot of them are very good, some of them not so good. Do the research and find one that fits the business.

Application

The first place that should be looked into for skip tracing information is the original application by the debtor, whether a corporation or individual. If the application is thorough and the credit personnel ensured accuracy and completeness of the application before processing, then the application itself will prove to be a source of good information. More often than not, there will be several bits of useful information on an application that do not make it into the account demographics on the computer. Pull it out and review the application.

Telephone Directory

This seems obvious, perhaps even outdated in today's day and age, but it is often overlooked for those very same reasons and it need not be. Searching the local telephone directory for the debtor can be the quickest and most cost efficient method of locating the debtor. Most would be surprised how many people are still listed in the phone book – it is still a very thick book.

Data Bases

There are many types of databases to use for the benefit of skip tracing. For example, there are multiple data bases sold for marketing purposes, which holds such information as names, addresses, phone numbers, places of employment, income levels, buying habits and the like. Credit reporting agencies are a very good example of useful databases; they provide very valuable information about a prospective or current customer. Many credit-reporting agencies sell database services aimed to assist the credit and collection professional and not only provide the business with the information they are looking for on the people the company is trying to find but they can offer the business a myriad of reports to help the company curb their risk.

There are other, many types of data bases to be discovered. Find the one appropriate for the company.

Not all databases require subscription fees, one that does not is the local courthouse. Most of the time, if the business has a serious delinquent debtor on their hands, chances are they are not the only one the debtor owes money too and it is very likely that other creditors have taken the debtor to court. The business can find all this information in the public records of the local courthouse. All the information about the debtor will be revealed and up to date as of the date of the court case.

Another source to try is the state agency that regulates business licenses in their state, their records are guaranteed to be as up to date as the most recent business filing update and can often provide the business with names and contact information for persons associated with the business that the business may not have been aware of.

Try local city offices. Sometimes useful information can be obtained from water departments or utility departments, however not always. What does seem to be easier to get information from are such departments as dog and fishing licenses bureaus, board of education records, city college boards and trade school enrollment departments.

Do not ignore the internet, obviously. Simply type in the name of the person or company who is being sought into Google. There are very few people, and almost no companies, that cannot be found in Google. Facebook and other social media are also useful.

CHAPTER EIGHT – LEGAL OPTIONS FOR CREDITORS

Credit and collections laws were made to protect the consumer; however, they were also enacted to give the creditor some legal resources in order to reduce their risk of carrying a defaulted portfolio. In order for creditors to take advantage of the assistance of the law, creditors must obey and follow the laws and regulations that govern creditors, adhering to them strictly; only by doing so will creditors be able to make use of the laws.

In any event, the debtor can and often does use the limits of the law to their advantage. Most debtors do not fully know the rights and laws that protect them as financial consumers, which is unfortunate, because it is those individuals who will be taken advantage of by less than lawful creditors. However, similarly, there are plenty of debtors that do know their rights and use them to every full advantage they can.

It is imperative as a creditor to know the key signs to watch for in order to prevent the company from falling into a legal trap that blocks the company from getting what is duly theirs.

Assignment For The Benefit Of Creditors

This is a good one; while on the surface it looks like the most beneficial and quickest way for the debtor to pay back creditors, it is not always and can be used to dupe the creditors.

An "assignment for the benefit of creditors" is an alternative to bankruptcy. How it works is, the debtor transfers all property and assets including receivables to another person or company, most of the time to an attorney. The then is given the duty of liquidating all assets and distributing all of the proceeds to the debtor's unpaid creditors. Any surplus is given back to the debtor.

A formal and court approved assignment for the benefit of creditors is granted at the request of the debtor without any consent of the creditor. The credit, however, will receive a written legal notice that the assignment has been granted. Once the creditor receives the written notice that the assignment has been set forth, the creditor is given so many days to file a proof of claim with the assignee. The way it is supposed to work is the assignee then sells all assets, property, receivables, tangible and intangible assets for the best possible price and then pays off the creditors. The assignee will keep a portion of the liquidated proceeds as his fee and another portion to cover the expenses of handling the assignment. Those will come out first, what is left will go to the creditors.

Unlike a bankruptcy, the use of an assignment for the benefit of creditors does not allow the creditor to examine the debtor or list of assets under oath, in fact the debtor can refuse to disclose such information, and therefore the use of the assignment is regulated very inefficiently. This remedy, the use of an assignment for the benefit of creditors, is very desirable to the less scrupulous debtor for obvious reasons. It is too easy to sell assets to a friend for pennies, then make use of the assignment, become free of debt, then require their assets back for pennies unscathed.

So what can the creditor do when they receive a notice that their debtor intends to put into place an assignment for the benefit of creditors? The creditors can file an involuntary petition for bankruptcy. In most cases, an involuntary petition for bankruptcy filed by a debtor's creditors will terminate the assignment for the benefit of creditors. If the company receives one such notice that their debtor has filed for an assignment, seek the court and obtain a list of creditors, contact those creditors and organize under a joint attorney to file an involuntary petition of bankruptcy for the debtor and stop the assignment. By doing so, the creditors can then examine the debtors assets and determine what has happened to them and if any were "hidden" in a "temporary sale."

Bulk Sales

A bulk sale occurs when a debtor sells all of his inventory and merchandise to one buyer outside the normal course of business; usually for less the value of retail and most usually for less than what is required to satisfy his creditors. In the past, a bulk sale would occur and the debtor would take the money, close his business and disappear with no monies paid to his creditors.

Most states today, however, have in place laws to regulate bulk sales in order to protect the creditors. It is required that the intended purchaser obtain a list of creditors from the debtor/seller and then notify them in writing of the date of the intended sale and the sale amount and the acknowledgement of whether or not the proceeds will be enough to pay off all of the creditors. In most cases, the buyer does not obtain the debts of the seller and if the bulk sale goes through leaving creditors unpaid then the creditors are left with little recourse.

One common trick that the debtor will do is before the announcement of the intended bulk sale, they will obtain a loan from a bank and use their inventory and merchandise as collateral. The debtor becomes insolvent and then obtains a purchaser for the remaining equipment and assets. The creditors are then notified of the bulk sale and informed they will not be paid off because the inventory is mortgaged and therefore owned by the bank.

Article 6 of the Uniform Commercial Code was written to protect the creditors from this type of bulk sale fraud. Most states have repealed Article 6 and replaced it with revised and updated acts. Company employees must become familiar with legislator in their state that replaced Article 6.

The article required that the buyer obtain a list of all creditors, notify them of the sale and all details and maintain this list of creditors for six months. They were also required to give this list to all auctioneers and others involved in the sale of the merchandise.

What this basically does for the creditor is that the old "call them not us" game whereas the creditor calls the debtor for payment only to be told they sold their business to the buyer and that they should call them for payment. When the creditor calls the buyer, they are told they only bought the assets and to call the buyer, and around and around it goes.

What does the creditor do in this situation? First of all, the bulk sale must be conducted under very strict rules, if it is not the creditors can seek to legally void the sale. If the bulk sale is being conducted with every legal and lawful intent, whereas the debtor incorporates no plan to defraud the creditors, then the debts owed by the seller to the creditors is outlined in the purchase contract and provisions are made to make good on those debts. Where this does not exist, the creditor should immediately and without hesitation seek legal counsel because the creditors are limited on the amount of days for response.

The bulk sales act is in place to protect the creditor, however it is up do the creditor to stay on top of the movements of their debtors and know when they are being defrauded. Injunctions can be filed to stop a bulk sale when the provisions of the sale will not make whole the creditors. Such instances can only be handled by an attorney.

Sale of Debtors Assets

In today's economy or in any economy really, it is very difficult for small businesses such as retail stores or restaurants to survive beyond the first few years. A lot of the time the reason for the demise of any small business is the lack of business shrewdness in the new owner; however, where one man or woman might not be able to make a go of it, another man or woman might be able to. In fact, it is common for small businesses to change ownership several times during its first decade and the customers generally never know. The unfortunate things is, usually the creditors do not know when the business is going to change hands.

Here is a common scenario: there is a vendor that makes and sells customized fast food containers and one of the clients is a local fast food hamburger joint that just opened up not too long ago, called Sol's Burgers. Like all new restaurants, the initial public interest of Sol's Burgers was big and the first few months, or perhaps the first year or two's sales were quite good. Then other burger joints open and the owners of Sol's, new to the world of managing a business, begin to get into the many complex aspects of running a business that they may not have experience with. Even a small hamburger joint will have serious accounting and management needs. For one reason or another, profits start to decline and Sol's owners feel they cannot make a go of it. However, Sol's Burgers is still making some profit and it has great potential, perhaps another owner could make a better run, so the owners of Sol's decide to sell the burger joint for more than they have put into it and make a nice little profit for themselves.

The business sells. The hamburger joint is now owned by someone else.

The receivables reports for the company that sells the customized fast food containers show that Sol's is now past due for the containers they bought three months back.

The vendor calls Sol's Burgers to collect payment and the call goes something like this:

Vendor: Hello, this is Rick with Gleam Containers, I am calling to speak to Sol.

Them: Sol is no longer here.

Vendor: Where is he?

Them: Sol no longer works here.

Vendor: I am sorry, I understand Sol is the owner of the restaurant. I have spoke to him several times.

Them: Sol is no longer the owner.

Vendor: To whom am I speaking?

Them: Olivia

Vendor: Olivia, may I please speak to the owners of Sol's Burgers.

Them: You are.

Vendor: I do not understand.

Them: I am Olivia, I bought Sol's Burgers from Sol last week. I am the new owner.

Vendor: As I stated, I am Rick from Gleam Containers and I am calling to collect $1,895 in past due receivables for containers shipped to Sol's Burgers May 28th.

Them: You will have to take that up with Sol. I am the owner of this restaurant as of August 15th. I am not liable for debt or expenses to Sol's Burgers before August 15th.

Cutting this conversation short, what arises from the remaining conversation is that Olivia bought Sol's Burgers from Sol, buying only the business, it's name and right to use the phone number and all identifiable aspects, Olivia bought the tangible and paid for assets but bought none of the credit purchased inventory or stock, therefore Olivia bought none of the debt. Olivia bought the business and assets but Sol maintained the debt and stock and inventory associated.

So what happened to Sol? Who knows? Let us say that Sol moved to Fiji and has not been heard from since. He lives in a grass hut with no phone, internet or mail service. He simply cannot be reached.

What are the vendor's options? In reality, there probably is not much that can be done. However, the monies paid by Olivia to Sol belong to Sol's creditors and basically Sol absconded with the monies owed to the creditors. When the sale of the business was conducted, it (more than likely) went through attorneys, escrow accounts or trusts. In other words, there is a legal paper trail of the sale.

Most creditors upon hearing that Sol's is under new ownership, and Sol cannot be reached, end their attempt at collecting right there. That is understandable, if Olivia is not legally liable for the debt and the vendor cannot reach Sol, the vendor seems to be out of luck.

There are two things however, that can be done in order to recover. The first thing is to contact the business' attorney. The attorney will need to contact the parties involved in the sale. When Sol's attorney set up the sale, did they make allowances for unpaid creditors? Was a list of creditors provided? If the business sold containers to Sol's Burgers on credit then the business has lien rights to the assets of the business. Certainly, collateral backed loans and credit accounts as well as UCC filings and mechanics and artists liens have precedence over non-collateral backed credit sales, however the rights to assets by the non-collateral backed creditors do not diminish in the wake. The vendor can seek a judgment suit to recover those assets from Sol and should do so. Of course, the company will have to weigh the cost of the suit against the unpaid balance and make the right financial decision as to which option is more profitable or arises in the least amount of loss, whether to pursue legal or not. In any event, the attorney that handled Sol's sale will most likely be able still get a hold of him. So at the very least, contact Sol's attorney and pursue contact with Sol to get that debt collected. File a judgment against Sol in order to garnish the amount due.

The second option the vendor has will be the more lucrative and it does not involve pursuing Sol at all. Who is Olivia using for containers? If the vendor did not know that the business sold, then logically it can be assumed that Olivia did not contact this vendor to set up a credit account for the purchase of her containers, therefore she must be using another vendor. Why? Most likely because she knew that Sol owed this vendor money.

Therefore, contact Olivia the new owner of Sol's Burgers again and get her business for containers. Tell her the credit of Sol's Burgers is still good with the company, all previous balances on the account have been wiped clean and the company is ready to ship those containers that Sol's has been using all along. Push the sales, collect the money and make up for the written off debt.

CHAPTER NINE – ACCOUNTING FOR BAD DEBT

Most understand the value of selling on credit. Most also understand that the more credit extended, the higher the risk of bad debt that there will be. This should not scare vendor away from selling on credit; it should, however, encourage the vendor to utilize the tools taught in this text to better control their accounts receivable risk. In doing so, they will not go wrong.

The following section is a basic over-view of how to account for bad debt in the books. For this purpose, the two most popular methods will be discussed: 1) the allowance method and 2) the direct-write-off-method.

Allowance Method

Bad debt expense is a loss from failure to collect on accounts receivable; be-it for whatever reason. The allowance method is a technique that will recognize the bad debt expense in the same period as the related sale. This technique goes hand-in-hand with the matching principle, which states that expenses should be matched with the revenues that created that expense, as the adage says, "you must have money to make money." The allowance method relates to that.

During usage of the accrual basis of accounting, the allowance method is generally required for financial reporting purposes. There are three basic steps to the allowance method:

1. At the end of each accounting period, the amount of uncollectible accounts is estimated.

2. An Adjusting entry is made to recognize the bad debt expense and reduce reported receivables for the amount of estimated uncollectible accounts.

3. In a subsequent period, when a specific uncollectible account is identified, an entry is made to write-off the account and reduce balance in allowance for bad debts.

In order to use the allowance method, the business does need a way to be able to estimate the amount of uncollectibles. There are two basic, more popular, methods for doing so: 1) the percent of sales method and 2) the percent of receivables method. Both methods are viable and useful, and will be historically accurate within their appropriate applications. The key to either method is to choose one and stick with it throughout.

Percent of Sales Method:

The percent of sales method is based on a reverse-collections notion; or better said, it is based on the idea that some percent of credit sales will need collections. This is a very true statement. In assuming the amount of credit sales that will not need collections, the company is then by default, then defining the percent of sales that will.

In order to apply the method, it is best to use historical data. The business can look back at their previous periods to determine the amount of bad debt that each period had historically. If this is the company's first year of operating, then the company will need to make their best educated guess based on the credit terms, relationships with the customers and the customer's credibility.

Value Based Management For Accounts Receivable

Assume $500,000 in period credit sales. Also assume that the historical records for that same period show an average of 2% bad debt. The journal entry for that period will look like this:

Bad Debt Expense $10,000

   Allowance For Bad Debt $10,000

Percent of Receivables Method:

The percent of receivables method is based on the notion that a certain amount of the company's period credit sales will go to collections. (Kind of the same thing as above, but the company is approaching it from the other end. Depending on the type of business, this may be a more realistic approach.)

To apply this method, it is necessary to focus on the relationship between the amount of accounts receivable at the end of the year and the amount of uncollectible accounts. The basic approach is to compute the uncollectible accounts as a percentage of the accounts receivable balance.

For example:

$$\frac{\text{Average Uncollectible Accounts}}{\text{Average Accounts Receivable}} = \frac{\$5,000}{\$100,000} = 5\%$$

The journal entry therefore would resemble the following:
'

Bad Debt Expense $5,000

   Allowance For Bad Debt $5,000

Although this method seems very simplistic in its approach, it can be somewhat imprecise. This is because with the approach, each dollar of accounts receivable is treated as having the same chance of being uncollectible. The previous sections of this book teaches this is not valid.. Some of the accounts will be higher risk than others. It is also the truth that the older a debt is, the harder it will be to get it collected.

For this reason, the percentage of receivables method can be applied in a way that better defines the percentage of uncollectible accounts. The company can do this by instead of using the total of accounts receivable, in the estimation formula, the company can analyze each customer's account to determine how long the amounts have been outstanding. Different percentages are then applied to the different amounts that have been outstanding for different amounts of time. This might seem daunting, but it is worth it. Because of the emphasis on the length of time debts are outstanding, this process is called aging the receivables.

Aging the Receivables:

If the company uses the aging of receivables method, they will no doubt be using a more accurate method of estimating accounts receivable bad debt. No matter how long the company have been in business, this is very important to controlling risk and increasing profitability.

To age the receivables:

1. Categorize each account receivable according to the length f time the amounts have been outstanding.

2. Multiply the amount of receivables in each category by an estimate of the percent that will be uncollectible. This percent is based on past experience and increases as the number of days past due increases.

3. Total the estimates for each category to determine the amount that is not expected to be collected.

To illustrate, we will use three accounts:

CUSTOMER	TOTAL	CURRENT	1-30	31-60	61+
Hill Co	$5,000	$3000	$2000		
James Co	$1000				$1000
Steven Co	$4000	$1000		$3000	

AGING BAD DEBT ESTIMATE

Total	$10000
Current	$4000 x 2% = $80
1-30	$2000 x 5% = $100
31-60	$3000 x 8% = $240
61+	$1000 x 30% = $300

The journal entry then, will resemble:

Bad Debt Expense $720
    Allowance For Bad Debt $720

Also, take a moment and note the aging bad debt estimate above. This is a good visual example of how the longer a debt goes unpaid, the more money it is costing the company. While the company can see that the amount of unpaid debt over time decreases in total dollars due, the amount of profit goes down over time by relation.

Writing Off Uncollectible Accounts:

Value Based Management For Accounts Receivable

Whether the company uses the percent of sales or receivables (aging) method, the journal entry to write off the debt looks the same:

Allowance for Bad Debt $4,582

  Accounts Receivable/Martinson Co $4,582

    Wrote Off Uncollectible Account

On the Balance Sheet, this will look like this:

Current Assets:

    Accounts Receivable $134,500

    Less Allowance Bad Debt $4,582

        Net Receivable $129,918

Direct-Write-Off Method

By contrast to the allowance method, the direct-write-off method states that bad debt expense is not recognized until it has been determined that an account is uncollectible.

The direct-write-off method has one clear advantage, in that it is very simple to apply. For that reason alone, the direct-write-off method is more often utilized by businesses over the allowance method. Even though it is the easiest and most popular method of the two discussed, the direct-write-off method does have its disadvantages.

The first disadvantage is that the activities conducted to collect accounts receivable, more often than not, will extend over multiple moths and therefore potentially across periods. Using the direct-write-off-method therefore, usually results in the revenue from the sale being recognized on one period while the corresponding bad debt write-off is recognized in another period.

Another disadvantage is that the amount of bad debt expense recognized in a given period can be creatively designed. The reason for this is that the decision as to when an account will be determined to be officially uncollectible can be subjective. In this manner, bad debt expense can be delayed by not showing accounts as bad debt when they should be.

The third disadvantage and a key disadvantage to the direct-write-off method is that the amount of accounts receivable that will be reported on the balance sheet will not be the actual amount of accounts receivable collected, and therefore, the balance sheet will not be truly accurate. This is because the direct-write-off method does not forecast uncollectible amounts in order to portray those amounts in the balance sheet. They occur when they occur, and while this might reflect a more positive capital base for the business, at the end of the year, the expected profit margin will be lower than expected. For this key reason alone, the direct-write-off method is generally not acceptable for financial reporting purposes and those companies utilizing it, if official financials need be prepared, those figures will have to be re-figured using the allowance method.

The journal entries for the direct-write-off method will look the same:

Allowance for Bad Debt $4,582

 Accounts Receivable/Martinson Co $4,582

  Wrote Off Uncollectible Account

When it has been determined and account is uncollectible, then it is written off. There are no estimations given.

Recovery of Previously Written-Off Accounts

It does happen that upon occasion, an account that had been previously written-off is newly collected.

If the business wrote it off, the business will have entered it thus:

Allowance for Bad Debt $4,582

   Accounts Receivable/Martinson Co $4,582

      Wrote Off Uncollectible Account

To Reinstate it:

Accounts Receivable/Martinson Co $4,582

   Allowance for Bad Debt Expense $4,582

      Reinstate Uncollectible Account

To Record Collection:

Cash $4,582

   Accounts Receivable/Martinson Co $4,582

      Collection on Account

CHAPTER TEN – CONCLUSION

In the end, it is important to note that the purpose of accounts receivable management is not to control the aging of unpaid debt; in truth, the purpose of accounts receivable management is to improve the profitability of the business itself. It may very well turn out that the business allows a certain amount of debt to go willingly to uncollectible write-offs because in doing so, this action creates a trade-off that increases sales by association and/or the very profit margin itself of those future sales.

Most every debt collection manager focuses on trying to collect more of the oldest aging at the expense of the profitability factor. Remember that the older the debt, the less money the business is making on it, even if the business does collect that sum.

The best activities of debt collection management are to be proactive and not reactive. A good debt collections manager spends more time on credit analysis and business relationship building than on collecting past due balances after the fact. If the collectors are making more outgoing phone calls to customers to collect past due accounts than they are receiving phone calls from the sales team to set up new accounts, the company needs to refocus their attention to the more up front tasks that will improve profitability by lowering risk.

Control risk = control accounts receivable.

There are so many accounts receivable blogs and editorials, both in print and on-line. Almost every one of them chants the same thing repeatedly: *call – call – invoice –send notices-call- call-invoice-send notices – the squeaky wheel gets the grease.* That is a reactionary stance that if followed, the company's DSO Profitability will be mediocre at best.

Utilize the information in this book as a guideline to help understand where to focus attention. Even if the business has been managing its own receivables for decades, now is the time to re-evaluate things. In fact, the longer that the business has been managing its own receivables, the more likely they are to need to revamp things. Be creative and look for those value driven solutions.